BENDING
THE RULES

✝

BENDING THE RULES

What American Priests Tell American Catholics

Jim Bowman

Introduction by
Andrew M. Greeley

CROSSROAD • NEW YORK

1994

The Crossroad Publishing Company
370 Lexington Avenue, New York, NY 10017

Printed in the United States of America

Library of Congress Cataloging-in-Publication Data

Bowman, Jim, 1931–
    Bending the rules : what American priests tell American Catholics
/ Jim Bowman ; introduction by Andrew M. Greeley.
        p.   cm.
    ISBN 0-8245-1360-6
    1. Catholic Church. Archdiocese of Chicago (Ill.)—History—20th
century. 2. Catholic Church—Illinois—Chicago—Clergy—Interviews.
3. Catholics—Illinois—Chicago—Religious life. 4. Catholic
Church—Illinois—Chicago—Discipline. I. Title.
BX1418.C4B68   1994
282'.7731—dc20   94-4120
                                                                                CIP

For Winnie and the Kids

Contents

Acknowledgments

- To the thirty-four priests who gave interviews.

- Mike Lenehan of the *Chicago Reader,* for help on chapter 1, which first appeared in that publication.

- To Frs. Andrew Greeley, Philip Kaufman, and Harvey Egan, all distinguished authors and veterans in the ministry, for their early, spontaneous encouragement.

- To Fr. Dick McCormick, S.J., for leading me to his collection of *Theological Studies* commentaries, gems one and all.

- To Betty, David, Fran, Frank, Gerry, Jim, Joe, and others who gave me leads.

Introduction

Compassion or Law?

by Andrew M. Greeley

I S CATHOLICISM a religion of law or compassion? The only possible answer is that it is both a religion of law and a religion of compassion, and that compassion is the more important of the two. In theory there ought to be no opposition between the two, and, as some of the priests trained in Rome explained to Jim Bowman, in practice, if one properly understands Roman law, there should be little if any conflict. However true that may be, those of us raised in the Anglo-Saxon/Celtic tradition feel that we encounter much conflict, even if it be only apparent conflict. The priests that Mr. Bowman has interviewed explain how they try to resolve the (apparent) conflicts. Clearly they choose in varying degrees for compassion. As they should.

It is my impression that these men represent the way most American priests would respond to such (apparent) dilemmas at the present time. I am intrigued by the fact that even before the Vatican Council some of these responses were possible, though rarely used. The so-called internal forum solution to certain marriage cases — between priest and parishioner outside of church courts, as in confession or counseling — was surely available, indeed, as a matter of right. Moreover, even in my day in the seminary (early 1950s) we were told of certain ways to get around the birth control problem. (A spouse could consent to contraceptive intercourse to save the marriage so long as he/she did not take the initiative in either the contraception or the particular act of contraceptive intercourse.) The difference between the pre-conciliar church and the post-conciliar church is that priests are far more likely to have recourse to such solutions now than they were then — and to be far more skeptical, not to say suspicious, of church authority.

11

If there is more (apparent) conflict between compassion and laws today the reason may well be that the distance between the Vatican and the lives of the ordinary laity seems to have become greater. Surely that is the problem about which someone ought to do something.

Like Bowman I am impressed by these priests. I agree with his judgment that many of them are noble men. Yet I also have reservations. Many (not all of them) are so deeply embedded in clerical culture that they do not realize how patronizing they can sound. The two that speak of the pedophile problem simply do not "get it." Like most priests they sympathize with other priests and seem unaware of the suffering of the victims and their families. The few priests who say that the laity are not "ready" for women priests and that the Catholic schools have done great harm are flat-out wrong. I was appalled by the priest who permitted his deacons to veto the use of women mass servers. Since when do deacons have the right to overrule the presiding officer of the parish liturgy, especially on a matter of fundamental human right?

I was surprised by how many of them had good things to say about their bishops, even though the bishops were conservative. Obviously many of the more conservative bishops have learned to adjust to the realities of the lives their priests must live. I was also surprised by how many of them had positive things to say about the pope; unlike them I feel his reign has been a disaster for the church.

Despite these misgivings I admire greatly most of the priests whom Bowman interviewed — to say nothing of my good friend, the perennially feisty Bishop William E. McManus. They are good priests doing their best in very difficult circumstances, far more flexible and humane than were many of their iron-fisted predecessors in the ages of brick and mortar. Many of the interviewees seem tired and discouraged, as well they might. I hope God gives them the strength and the health to continue their compassionate work and that She also shouts in the ears of church leaders that they should wake up and listen to men like these.

Christmas Eve 1993

BENDING
THE RULES

Chapter 1

Bending the Rules:
The State of the Question

MICHAEL-TOO-GOOD-TO-BE-TRUE, young and educated and willing, comes to see Fr. John White, veteran pastor of St. Calliope's, a seven-hundred-family racially mixed Chicago parish. He wants to join the parish and take some responsibility for its success. Everything about him is appealing: he's educated and articulate, committed to the church, leads a well-organized life as a productive citizen and responsible family man. Trouble is, he has what's called in Catholic circles "a bad marriage."

Fr. White can welcome him to the fold and sign him up for the parish committee of his choice, pasting his address to a box of his very own collection envelopes. Or he can politely tell the bright young prospect, who not incidentally also has a soul to be saved, to get lost.

"It's a matter of taking him in or sending him away," says Fr. White, who's been at this kind of work for thirty-six years. "But if you want to take him in, you have to forget about canon law."

That's what Fr. White does. He forgets about canon law and takes Mr. Too-Good-to-Be-True in, him and his wife and kids. He "regularizes" the couple's marriage on his own, bypassing chancery and marriage court. Mr. T. becomes a member in good standing, with benefit of clergy.

That's what dozens of other Catholic priests do too in Chicago, to judge from what he and four other parish veterans

15

testified in closed session about how things are done in the rectories and visitors' parlors of that far-flung archdiocese.

They bend church law to meet pastoral needs. Representing a centuries-old institution hoary with precedent and known for its hard public line on sex, marriage, and related matters, they are also pastors trained to be nice guys when the occasion presents itself.

"There is no reason for someone walking away without being reconciled in some way," says Fr. Tom Green, eighteen years a priest, pastor of a 275-family "struggling" black inner-city parish. "If not on the spot, then after a pastor has worked with them and their conscience."

His name isn't Green, no more than White's is White. Their names, and those of others quoted here, are changed to protect the guilty and their endangered ministry. "Keep this law-bending anonymous," said one, "because if it were known, it would be stopped."

They would be called in and told to cease and desist by their archbishop, Cardinal Joseph Bernardin, who would feel obliged to set them straight, no matter how much experience they have. To them it's a matter of common sense and compassion; to him, or at least to people he must take into careful consideration, it's deviant behavior of the first water.

A bad marriage is a second marriage "attempted" while the first marriage is still legal. In civil life that's bigamy, but here it's only adultery because the church does not recognize the second marriage at all. There is no second marriage. None. Nil. *Nada. Pas de mariage. Nicht.* It's living in sin. The partners can't take communion. The offspring are illegitimate. If the sons ever want to be ordained priests, the pope's permission is required, so as to lift the burden of bastardy. It is heavy stuff, posing the knottiest of questions to the compassionate, commonsensical everyday, garden-variety parish priest, the kind quoted here.

There's annulment, of course — of the first marriage — or "Catholic divorce" as it's known. Even then it's a "declaration of nullity," which is to say an official judgment that the first marriage never existed.

Annulment procedures aren't what they were in the early 1950s, when it took "proof of forced marriage, and then before a marriage was consummated, or impotence," said Fr. George

Grey, thirty-six years a priest, pastor of an eighteen-hundred-family, mostly white-ethnic suburban parish. "Now 'psychic impotence' is the norm, something completely different."

Psychic impotence is of the mind and heart. The marriage partner is judged to have been immature or worse at the time of the wedding, incapable of taking on and living up to the commitment.

Annulments? They're given out "like popcorn," said Fr. Grey. "People know that. We had a guy married twenty-two years. Divorced and remarried, his first marriage was declared null. If he could, anyone can. People sense that."

"Some accept annulment-seeking as a game," said Fr. Brown, forty-five years a priest and associate pastor in a blue-collar parish of twenty-seven hundred families. "I don't think anybody believes in annulment."

Fr. Grey gives his own annulments. "I say to myself, if the diocese gives annulments, so can I. One of our best parishioners faced a year and a half delay. I thought, She'll get one in a year and a half? I'll give it to her now."

He witnesses the marriage and records it in church books, ignoring the previous marriage. "I don't do it often," he said. "I'm not 'Marryin' Sam.' And one of these days, I know damn well, I'm gonna get caught."

It's not for a younger, less experienced priest to decide, said Fr. Brown, who considers Fr. Grey qualified to make such decisions. Fr. Brown makes them too. He tells people, "If you want a small ceremony, come to the parlor and get a blessing. If you want a big one, go downtown," meaning to the chancery, where they get their annulment.

"If we only had thought of this thirty-five years ago," said Fr. Grey, who remembers the dozens of black Catholics, some like Michael Too-Good-to-Be-True, who were turned away because of bad marriages.

Fr. White agreed. "As priests, we're here to promote goodness, not pass judgment, not condemn and tell people what they can and cannot do," he said. "That's malarkey."

Their position is standard operating procedure for many parish priests. Of seven parishes in one cluster, only one does not handle marriages this way, said Fr. Brown. The rest "are at the cutting edge," that is, willing to cut corners.

In another part of town, it's the same story, even among priests who hew to the line in other matters they don't believe in — like blessing throats in February, thought to ward off respiratory ailments, no small thing in Chicago in the winter.

The "regularized" second marriage is justified because times have changed, argues Fr. Grey. It admits people to communion, because there is no longer "scandal" at what they have done, and giving scandal is what disqualified the communicant in church law.

"Divorce is culturally accepted. There's no rationale in church law for keeping people from communion, only in tradition based on the law. Anyhow, in this matter the only one who can say if the person is wrong is the person himself. Meanwhile, people are hurt. The divorced and remarried just forget about the church."

Birth control and abortion almost never come up. People don't ask. "The church did a good job teaching people about using their consciences when it came to birth control," said Fr. Thomas Black, twenty years a priest, referring apparently to churchmen like himself. On the "A-question," abortion, people are already convinced and range from "abortion clinic bombers" to "doers without hesitation."

Papal authority is a problem in itself. "Our people, who are well educated, are aware of the pope, but among them his popularity is zilch," said Fr. Grey. "They're openly critical, especially as regards birth control and remarriage after divorce. They say, 'He's crazy, who cares about him?'"

A lesser-known conflict has been over group "reconciliation," the sacrament of reconciliation (formerly Penance, or just "going to confession") without confessing to a priest.

Fr. Brown's blue-collar parish has group or communal reconciliation services twice a year, for thirty-five hundred at a time from six parishes. The same six have three other services a year in other churches. Reconciliation services are worlds apart from the one-on-one, sometimes bleak experience of individual confession in a darkened confessional, or "box," a wardrobe-sized enclosure with kneeler and screened opening. Through the opening one talks to the priest, who is for some reason called the confessor, though he mostly listens.

Nowadays the confessional is largely an antique, something

toddlers try to get into during long sermons when the father or mother has taken the kid out of the pew before terminal squirming got to them both. Or something CCD (Sunday-school) kids are shown as part of their tour of the premises.

The confessional had long fallen into disuse when church worship experts came up with what seems to be a viable substitute, namely, this reconciliation service with lights, music, and the company of one's neighbors. At such a service, having preached and prayed and led in prayer and song, a squad of priests give "absolution," or divine forgiveness, to thousands at a time. Then each lay person comes to the front to receive one by one the "laying on of hands," which more or less confirms the process.

The service is a communal acknowledgment of sinfulness, said Fr. Brown, clearly excited about the procedure, rather than the private recounting of one's recent history to the priest acting as judge and granting absolution.

At issue is whether the centuries-old requirement of individual confession may be ignored in favor of something that "works" pastorally — that is, achieves in a different way what the old system can't. This communal forgiveness has been officially reserved for emergencies, like imminent shipwreck or battle. Authorities would stop the practice as Fr. Brown described it; indeed he urgently asked that his parish's identity be kept secret.

But he and his fellows also feel the need to justify what they do. They may be free-lancers or incipient congregationalists. But they are conscientious free-lancers. So they ask the opinion of a sympathetic theologian, who didn't want to be identified either, such is the pressure from above in these matters. The theologian gave them a rationale for what they do, thus tying them in with tradition, and their consciences are clear.

Other experts, canon lawyers, worked out (in the semi-public forum of learned journals) a rationale for the psychic-incapacity annulment. Each expert served as a sort of rabbi, you might say, interpreting the law. Jews and Catholics have more in common than they realize.

The reconciliation service provides a great sense of community, says Fr. Brown. This is its attraction, he thinks, but he and his colleagues aren't sure. He talks about it like a man in search of what works: you try this, you try that. You don't sit still or rest on laurels. Somewhere there's the perfect service.

What they have preserves both public and private aspects of the sacrament, he says, again as one who measures until he has it right. The public part is strictly Vatican II. Very few Catholics before that time thought there was supposed to be anything public about confession. It was between God and sinner — oh, and that disembodied voice in the darkness, beyond that screen.

Their theologian showed them how to get at both sides, the public with the communal service, the private with the laying on of hands. They told him what they were doing, and he gave his *imprimatur*, you might say.

It's a church where law and tradition matter, but where the official interpreters aren't always well versed in either. The priests want theological and historical grounds on which to defend their actions. They draw on "the history of moral theology," as Fr. Brown put it, the better to understand the law as written for today's church.

A pastor's decision to bury the dead can provoke another crisis, or at least irritation. Suicides or people married outside the church or resigned priests married without church permission are all officially to be refused Catholic burial. Nonetheless, most pastors would bury any and all of these, said Fr. Black.

Beneath all these issues simmers the question of law and its role in the church. These priests don't want to flaunt their flouting of the law, nor do they consider it out-and-out flouting, for that matter. But neither do they consider the law sacrosanct. "When the law does not serve people, the law should be changed," said Fr. White, after all echoing the Founder, who had something to say about for whom the Sabbath was made and for what man (read people) was not.

Nonetheless, there's another small problem. When law stays put but practice goes its own way, what about honesty? What to do about the gap between public, official proclamation and private, unofficial practice?

"We priests proclaim both the hard and the compassionate sayings of Jesus," said Fr. Green. "The institutional church preserves the hard sayings. But the pastoral side — meeting one to one with a priest — emphasizes the compassionate side. But that's never made public. The public side preserves the hard line. It used to, anyhow. Now it's getting fuzzy. Dissent is more publicized. Even learned articles, once the preserve of professionals, are more widely read. People have their own ideas."

Some, on the other hand, "are suspicious when they hear of the tradition of the compassionate pastor," said Fr. Green. "It's been a semi-secret. Now it's in the open."

But "compassion was taught in the seminary," Fr. Brown said. Among other things seminarians learned the principle of *epikeia* (Greek for "reasonableness"), which requires bending the letter of the law to fulfil the lawmakers' intent. In practice, he said, it means "You can forgive anything, but don't make it public."

He told the story of the East Coast cardinal-archbishop who years ago prescribed for his priests a hard line on birth control, shortly after publication of *Humanae Vitae*, the 1968 papal encyclical forbidding it. A young priest worried aloud about how difficult it would be for him to withhold absolution (forgiveness) in confession. "Refuse absolution?" said the archbishop in horror, and this in front of a large gathering of his priests. "I've been a priest forty years and I've never done that." The cardinal's public position had to be hard-line. His pastoral approach was something else.

Fr. Grey says it's dishonest to maintain the image of the church as all-knowing when it isn't. That has to change. "It means saying less and claiming less. We are not nearly as sure as we once were. We have to learn to live comfortably with that."

A complicating factor is the changing profile of the priesthood. Priests in their forties, fifties, and sixties generally look back on Vatican Council II as a watershed in their experience of the church. But younger priests, many formed by reaction to Vatican II rather than by the council itself, often lack a Vatican II vision and are "much more conservative," said Fr. White.

"It's a national situation," said Fr. Brown.

Most lay people, on the other hand, though not all, accept change as a regular thing. Some seem to yearn for the authoritative institution of old. They look for guidance and want it specific, even seem eager to see dissenters punished.

It's a matter of growing up, says Fr. Grey, "like forgiving your parents for not being perfect. Once we do that, we can love them as adults. We were taught the church is perfect, but we see it now as a human institution inhabited by God."

Better to face up to the old man's or old lady's failings, even when she's Mother Church, he says, than leave her cold. "The church can make hash of things. It has done so for centuries. We rejoice when it does well, grieve with it at other times. But we don't leave it, because we have learned how to forgive it."

Where then does authority reside? "In our deepest wisdom," he said, enunciating a view of the matter that, it is safe to say, many an old monsignor would not have enunciated fifty years ago.

"Sometimes in church authority, sometimes in the community of faith, where consensus of the faithful leads us to the truth. The greatest wisdom is no longer expected from celibate clergy but from people's life experience. It's not clear-cut. We must wrestle with it."

The faithful are up to it, he and the others feel. A parishioner asked Fr. Brown if he could take communion at a Lutheran church, where a friend was getting married. Brown told him, "It's against the rules. But if it was a close friend of mine, I'd do it."

"Thanks, Father," the man said. "I'll do it and leave it up to God."

Chapter 2

What the Priests Were Asked

THE FIRST GROUP OF PASTORS, Chicagoans, had their say in chapter 1. Coming up are interviews with twenty-nine more veterans who tell how they function in the world of the parish. Almost all bend rules in one way or another, or at least admit to the reality. All have twenty or more years' experience. Ten have over thirty years, two have over forty, one over fifty. One is a bishop; all are or have been pastors.

Most chose to be anonymous. The option was offered to all because of fears expressed by the first group of being penalized if their views and practices became known. Another reason became clear during the second wave of interviews, namely, that parishioners were involved, and so discretion was in order.

So the interviewees are disguised in most cases, for two very good reasons: if they weren't, they would be punished or at least severely inhibited in their ministry, and their clients deserve anonymity too.

But the world deserves their candor. Sores fester beneath the body politic when not exposed. So with the body ecclesiastic. In truth, more good things than festering sores are brought to light in these pages — marvelous stories and statements of noble goals and aspirations. But there are problems too, as the reader will discover.

And solutions. That's the wonderful thing about letting priests let their hair down: you expose yourself to an almost dying breed of principled and idealistic men (men only, and that's a problem) who leap for the opportunity to talk about their work.

They are educated, dedicated, motivated, even as they function in various stages of deterioration, weariness, even, as one accused himself, of paranoia.

One is the author of a book to which this book might conceivably stand as a companion volume: *Diary of a City Priest* (Sheed and Ward, 1993). He is Fr. John P. McNamee, who finds himself blessed by not having to bend rules. Fr. John is a throwback. His book is confessional, a literary form in which men and women of the West have engaged and indulged for hundreds of years. He also lives a lonely, celibate, praying life and practices ministry on a largely person-to-person basis without benefit of super-organization, community, or otherwise. He's not a social worker or community organizer. He's a pastor full of doubts and belief.

Some of the interviewees are long past whatever *delicatesse* would forbid commentary on the record about bishop and even fellow priests, though none is crabbed. They talk and are named, per agreement, in some cases having already said publicly what they say here, one way or another.

Some are so much in the thick of it they can't countenance being known. One says he's sneaky. On his way out the door, he checks to be sure it's anonymous. Too much is at stake. It's not just being called on the carpet, with the emotional and time-wasting bother of it all; it's the work itself. They could be shut down. The organization would move to protect itself. So they must protect themselves against the organization.

It happens. Ask teachers or doctors or assembly-line workers or airline pilots. Almost everybody has something to lose by candor. And yet if they didn't bend the rules, what would happen? One theory is that the best way to bring an organization to its knees is to go entirely by the book. Indeed, haven't there been work stoppages or slowdowns based on union members' unbending observance of the contract?

There's not a book of rules written that can cover everything, as the pastors say one way or another time and again. If you love your organization, then for God's sake use your head! Bend the rules.

To Catholics with too reasonable and logical an approach to their church, what these pastors say may come as a relief. Some knew it all along, that their priests were using common sense and sensitivity to handle the problems of the day. Others didn't, and don't.

Some may be shocked or offended by what the priests say. Many others will be relieved. What they read will come as a booster shot for their struggling belief and loyalty. Sure, Fr. Jones has a nice touch. He saved the day for Aunt Lucy, stuck in her bad marriage. Or Fr. Smith must have said something right to our teenage son, who is not so surly lately. But we didn't know it was *common* for priests to be so sensible.

The admirable Smith and Jones may have bent the rules. This book is about how priests bend rules to make the church work for its members, who Vatican II told us *are* the church.

Some procedural matters. Each interviewee in the chapters that follow was given chapter 1 and a questionnaire, usually before the interview. Some received these items after a telephone interview, which they chose to do on the spot, without ado. All had the option of reading the materials first.

Not everybody consented, with or without anonymity. Eighteen declined. One had been "burned once" by plain speaking; another saw himself as "adding nothing." Another chuckled and said no, but added that he looked forward to reading the book. Another, once a firebrand, said he now "thinks with the pope" and "that's my happiness" now.

Another wanted no part of "church-bashing." Another, serving a big Hispanic community whose people "love the pope" and simply "skip communion" if they practice birth control, said the issues to be discussed are "middle-class" and of no concern to people at the low end of the socio-economic spectrum.

Another had been burned benignly by a glowing newspaper account that left him flooded with correspondence and donations, every one of which he returned with a letter of explanation! Enclosing people's cut-in-half checks, he explained that he hadn't intended to solicit donations in the article, which he considered a romanticizing of himself, and furthermore, they should not donate to causes they know so little of! Where do we locate this gentleman in the galleries of honest men?

Many were too busy. Several were put off by reading chapter 1, even after buying into the project sight unseen, supplying helpful insights in on-the-spot phone conversations.

Tone tells, perhaps. At least one chapter 1 reference, to annulment as "Catholic divorce," was called "flippant" by one interviewee.

Fair enough. The questions were pointed. Some interviewees objected to some, and said so. Most found most questions useful. All found the process interesting and many seemed to enjoy it. Why not? Someone comes asking how they do their life's work, listening, recording, taking notes.

It's flattering, and meant to be so. The questioner takes their life work seriously, hangs on every word, is fascinated by their combination of sense and sensibility, finds himself refreshed by every one of these interviews. This was good duty, let it be said.

Some years back, I did the same with a bunch of physicians, for the history of a medical center, and had the same reaction. These are, frankly, cream-of-the-crop types doing interesting and valuable work that is full of problems that they try honestly to solve. Isn't that a formula for fascination?

To the questions, then. Andrew Greeley told me years ago that a journalistic survey I had in mind would be interesting and useful. Coming from a working sociologist, this meant a lot. I was a daily newspaper reporter, probing and poking for what would interest a then-vast newspaper audience. It was my business not to break ground in learned journals but to grab and keep the interest of a fairly intelligent general reader.

Greeley probably forgets he told me that years ago. But it stayed with me. He and his fellow number-crunchers at the University of Chicago would nail down a thesis, verifying it to within their favorite three or four percentage points either way. But who knows what insights or creative focusing might come from a dumb reporter asking obvious questions?

So this is neither sociology nor ecclesiology nor pastoral theology nor catechetics nor moral theology nor a groundbreaking study of canon law. It's rather a journalistic essay, largely in interview form. These were the questions:

1. *Birth control:* How do you handle it, or do you? What do you say about this, the most widely rejected teaching of all?

2. *Abortion:* What do people ask? Do they ask? What is your pastoral experience in the matter, your abortion ministry or anti-abortion ministry?

3. *Marriage and divorce:* How often do you run into "bad marriages"? What do you do about them?

4. *Altar girls and women's ordination:* Do you have altar girls? Have you discussed the matter with your bishop? How does the "women question" arise in your ministry and how do you respond?

5. *Gay and lesbian issues:* How, if at all, do they turn up in your ministry? What do you say or do?

6. *Liturgy:* Do you employ unauthorized innovations for the sake of pastoral effectiveness? How do you justify this?

7. *Pope as hero, pope as goat:* How do you look on the pope and the papacy? Do you feel disloyal to him? How do others feel?

8. *The liberal-radical argument:* Assuming your own idealism and your willingness to forget law in varying degrees, letting the spirit move you, where do you fall on a radicalism spectrum? Where do you think others fall? (As idealists, the priests face fundamental law-vs.-freedom questions. As rule-benders, they are drawn in varying degrees to anti-law positions. The question probes this presumed tendency, which has been espoused by some Catholics in quasi-revolutionary fashion.)

9. *Obedience to authority:* Do you employ subterfuge for the common good? Defy the bishop? Do others? Do you fear retaliation?

10. *A fantasy:* What if pastors held to a hard line? Would a happy few congregate in moral and doctrinal purity? Would churchgoing sink to European levels?

These being the questions, what were the answers? In general — and I hesitate to sum them up because of the variety — they were these:

1. Birth control came off as the great solved mystery. Nobody asks, nobody asks, nobody asks. Time and time again.

People have voted perhaps with their feet but more likely with their consciences. Priests bring it up, sometimes worried about the big family with mother at church and father confused and bewildered, both victimized by loyalty to church gone wrong, sometimes to anticipate doubts or guilt when the young couple faces family-limitation problems down the road.

2. Abortion? After the fact, after the fact, after the fact, sometimes many years later. No priest classes abortion with birth control, but all clearly put their pastoral guard up when the penitent arrives. Bent on full reinstatement, they throw no stones, especially in these tragic cases with their potential for repeating themselves. Some also, surprisingly, lean toward accepting abortion in cases of rape or incest.

3. Marriage and divorce is the chief rule-bending arena. Most of these priests adjust to what's not amenable to legal solution. Annulment yes, delays yes, paperwork yes within limits. But if no annulment, then what? Then it's time to discern the reality and offer the way out. Many offer it; many take it. "Catholic divorce," that controverted term, occurs in people's heart of hearts, it seems, as often as or more often than in the marriage courts. This is the "internal forum" mentioned by Greeley in the introduction. It's a face-to-face extra-judicial situation involving priest and parishioner in confession or in counseling.

4. Altar girls seem standard. The U.S. bishops asked permission when they needn't have done so; permission hasn't arrived; it's time to cut losses and get on with the mass.

Women's ordination is a lost cause for this generation, and some of these priests confess their inability to convince women staffers and others who chafe at what they consider unconscionable delay. The priests agree to the unreasonableness of it. Some urge alternative measures for now, lest impatient women become obsessed with the issue. Most keep reminding people about this churchwide injustice.

A fair number moved directly into the priest shortage question at this point, bemoaning their overworked plight and making their case for ordination of men and women, married or otherwise.

5. Gays and lesbians are often hidden church members. All these priests show "compassion" toward them in their situation, which many attribute to genetics. More than a few say perma-

nent partnerships are a good alternative. Some "bless houses" of partners. One stresses the importance of a low profile in ministry to gays and lesbians.

Some are concerned about what they consider a disproportionate number of gays among priests. Some praise their gay priest friends. One preached a much-remembered sermon at the funeral of his best friend, an AIDS victim. But there's a problem here, say the concerned ones, not unrelated to mandatory celibacy and its reliance on the unmarried.

6. Liturgy discussions were rather surprising, in that illegal innovations are mostly in ill repute. Only the general absolution issue is alive, and that's a fence-sitter, it seems, not clearly unauthorized at all. But for most, liturgy is like Christianity in G. K. Chesterton's phrase: it has not been tried and found wanting; rather, it hasn't been tried. It's a rich source, with many largely untapped possibilities, say many.

7. The pope, ah, the pope! There's great appreciation for his traveling papacy, his ability to sway crowds, his performance as a unifying symbol. But in all this, he's an icon rather than a spokesman for them. For one priest, the most outspoken on this point though not on others, he is an obstacle to pastoral success, something this priest feels he has to live down in the day-to-day. A number resent his authoritarianism, which they consider a betrayal or at least forsaking of Vatican II goals. And the bishops he appoints! Spare us, they say, not that they are all bad. Conservatism isn't the issue here. Being "pastoral" covers a multitude of doctrinal crotchets.

8. Liberals and radicals? Comments here cover a lot of ground. "The gospel is radical, so am I" is one of them. And let it be noted that these priests are much enamored of the gospel. Is this a gospel church or isn't it? That is the question. Others emphasize their strength in numbers, saying, "I'm no maverick." Most took a crack at this largely open-ended question. Why? I think it's because they are thinking men.

9. Authority? Here the gospel looms large. Obedient, yes, they say, but to whom or to what? In the end, many have to turn to their consciences and their Lord, though most say they have not been forced to defy anyone. Still, there are times when bishops move in strange ways, and the pastor has to draw the line.

10. The fantasy about a church that bends no rules: Some say they would quit. It's not their kind of church, and they would want no part of it. Others are less clear about what this church would look like. One wonders what that hard line would be, in effect rejecting the fantasy as too fantastic.

One talks of the underground church that would develop in response. He seems the most hopeful of all, looking to a day when pope and bishops are repressive, inspiring priests and people to be more creative. In this view, the church is the people, and you can't keep a good church down. A bully notion.

Chapter 3

Preface to the Interviews

THESE INTERVIEWS are ordered according to a deeply mystical process that the author cannot reveal, closely akin to throwing students' papers down a staircase and giving grades based on how high they land.

The chief guide, to be frank and honest, has been to mix 'em up, like a junk-ball pitcher. Keep the reader slightly off balance. Do not let her decide, "Ah, that's what he's up to, I get it, on to the next book."

Not to say there is intent to confuse. Far from it. What I am counting on is that the reader catch some of the excitement I felt while (a) interviewing these priests and (b) editing the interviews.

The interviewing is seductive, to be sure. You sit across the table from a man who keeps hundreds, even thousands, spellbound on Sunday, and just because it's Tuesday is he tongue-tied and powerless? No, and the sympathetic interviewer is vulnerable. It's still a nice way to start.

The editing and rereading is something else. Many's the time while doing it I have burst out laughing or yelling and clapped my hands at how that man said it — the humor of it, the insightfulness, the nobility, the ... Hold on there. These guys put on pants a leg at a time.

But if you ask enough questions, you come up with the right question at the right time in the right way, and they dig deep and come up with something. I am prejudiced in favor of those closer questions (in the closing-innings sense, to keep the junk-baller motif), the ones about being radical or liberal, favoring or disfavoring the pope, employing subterfuge, fantasizing about a universal hard-line church.

They dug deep on those questions, and I am eternally grateful. And I use the term as one who expects there is an eternity. This is forever, folks. All things pass, we know. But we do make our mark, and I am extremely grateful to these gentlemen. They gave me (us) their time. I think they liked doing it. I am confident it was a good thing they did.

As to aliases, I got most of them from a wonderful medium-size volume called *Dictionary of Fictional Characters* (The Writer, Inc., 1977), which has names to spare. Wagstaff, for instance, has turned up four times in English and American novels since 1857, though once with an "e" on the end. Michael Wagstaffe was a "pseudo-American assassin" in a 1920 novel, *These Charming People*. No similarity intended, of course, to the Fr. Wagstaff of these interviews, who is nobody's assassin and is, I think, distinctly American.

The main advantage this *Dictionary* offered was ease of discovery. All those names and just enough time. A lesser advantage was that they are mostly English names, not Irish or other ethnic. I liked that because we ethnics are so easily categorized. Or were, when we were mostly immigrants or immigrant types. Now not even the immigrants are immigrant types.

The world and the nation have changed, and so has our church. This judgment turns up here and there in the interviews. We are characterized as no longer an immigrant church. And so we are not. Not even priests with ties to Ireland come across as Irish. For that matter, it may be that not even the Irish do any more.

In any event, by their aliases you will not know them. And you will know they are aliases by the generic, stingy description of their provenance and venue, to throw in a bit of French derivation while we are at it. Do the French still sound French, by the way? An interesting question, no doubt betraying a certain latent Midwest provincialism.

What else?

Most interviews dispense with quotation marks, providing responses in first-person, Sergeant Friday style (of TV "Dragnet" fame). Several use quote marks, including the two that involved more than one priest. It would have looked like a play script otherwise.

The others that use quotes, *à la* your standard newspaper story, may be explained in one of several ways. One, mystically, as the order of interviews was explained. Two, as being obviously demanded by the subject matter, which obviously demanded it (harrumph). Three, in the words of the school-boy penitent explaining to an impatient priest why he had committed a mortal sin, "It seemed a good idea at the time."

The subheads are a reporter's shot at being a headline-writer. In my experience at one of our late, great newspapers, headline-writers did a very good job of it. Here was my chance to emulate them, to highlight "what's to come." Alas, the subheads are about as imaginative as encyclopedia headings.

That was the idea. Organized this way, the book is easier to dip into. I met a bishop friend some weeks back and told him what I was about, glowingly. We stood with drinks in our hands in a seminary dining room. I was full of my project and told him about it, and while doing so — tentatively, meekly — came out with a characterization of this book as just maybe a sort of anecdotal manual of pastoral theology. One of my interviewees was kind enough to speculate in that direction. I was not eager to dispel the impression.

In any event, if it's a manual, it deserves easy-access format, and that's where the subheads come in.

What we have here is not, I hope, Cool Hand Luke's failure to communicate. What we have is professional commentary by veterans who have survived all sorts of comings and goings in the last twenty to fifty years and were kind enough to tell a few trade secrets. Is the seminarian or other pastor in training or working pastor curious about what these men say? Let her or him look.

Chapter 4

Fr. Wagstaff: Common Sense

FR. MIKE WAGSTAFF heads a suburban parish of seventeen hundred families in an old Midwestern community where everybody knows everybody else's business. One of its five weekend masses is in Spanish. The range is working class to professional. He is nearing his thirtieth anniversary as a priest.

His ordination followed prep seminary and the full major seminary program. He grew up in a solid Catholic family, medium size for its time, big by today's standards.

He remembers a boyhood incident that provided one source of his notions about church rules and regulations. It was when his father, at mass when Mike was ten years old, casually picked up the host that had fallen to the floor during communion time.

Normally this required a solemn high rescue operation, but his father, raised in an Eastern rite, where edges are less sharp, just picked it up and handed it to the priest, saying, "Here it is, Father."

"We thought his hand would fall off," recalled Mike, speaking for his brothers and himself, Catholic grade school students.

Even so, Mike saw it as "simple, direct, good," because it was done "so reverently and with common sense."

That's the trouble, he said. "Common sense gets short shrift in the Catholic Church." He aims at applying common sense to his pastoral work, "not being tied up in procedure and practices."

His own development as a pastor began in the seminary in the early 1960s, where a few read the German Jesuit theologian

Karl Rahner on their own but most, he included, spent their time "playing basketball and passing tests."

He feels it was "a fortunate time," between the old and the new, what with the Second Vatican Council meeting during his time of theology studies. "We knew the old theology and practice but didn't take it seriously. We knew it didn't offer the answers or even ask the questions. But neither did we want to put down what the old guys did."

He came out of the seminary "not questioning much." His first parish assignment was in a university community. "We had Jesuits living with us," he recalled. It was "a stimulating place."

But most important, the community exposed him to non-believers and Jews and Protestants, "wonderful people of all different beliefs," some in the peace or civil rights movements. He had dealt almost exclusively with Catholics, but here were people "in touch with the human struggle, what life's about." There was "something good in it, whatever you wanted to label it."

One book in particular "said things I was thinking and feeling," he recalled — the Canadian theologian Gregory Baum's *Man Becoming.* "It made so much sense to me. I could understand almost everything he said. That sort of thing shapes your approach to discipline and practices."

Birth Control

He endorses the recent comment by his "favorite bishop," Kenneth Untener, of Saginaw, Michigan, to the effect that Pope Paul VI's encyclical reaffirming the birth-control ban, *Humanae Vitae,* was "an old road map" for a terrain now with "new roads." "Same starting point, same destination," said Mike. "But common sense tells us that the old route is not the best."

Start then with birth control, the bone that never made it down for Catholics:

"In my ministry it doesn't come up. But I bring it up," to clear the air, as it were. In marriage preparation sessions, he asks the couple what they have been told in pre-Cana or Cana sessions. They say they have heard about "natural birth control," a sophisticated rhythm method. But in any case, it's "not a troubling thing" for them.

"I explain that there's a division in the church. The official position is against it, but there's division on the matter. I tell them that after some thought they can follow whatever opinion seems true and real and good for them.

"I make it clear there's no infallibility involved here. None seem hesitant or questioning, but I feel obliged to explain a little, because they are going to hear about it later, somewhere. Sometimes I say it was a troublesome issue for their parents or grandparents. I try to give them a basis for figuring it out."

Abortion

As for abortion, "surprisingly, it's not much of an issue," he said. He and other priests he has worked with over the years "have never been strong in pro-life activities." He has "even preached a couple times that while I believe abortion is wrong, I don't think we need all the legal blocks" urged by the pro-life movement and the bishops themselves.

"It's a pluralistic society, and a lot of good Christians and believers think abortion is okay on certain occasions."

"You don't condemn, you try to persuade," he said, quoting Cardinal Joseph Bernardin of Chicago. On the other hand, pro-life activists are "fierce and prone to condemn."

On his parish's staff now is a young priest who is starting a pro-life group. Mike appreciates his approach. "He asks us priests. He's not pushy at all, realizing there are different opinions and that we have to be respectful of each other."

But in general, his parish has not done much "about abortion." At election time, "we feel we should say something when people come with a list, telling who's for, who's against abortion, and want us to vote that way. I feel it's a very narrow approach, and say so."

On the personal level, "people come back ten years after" having an abortion, to confession. He is vaguely aware that once it was a sin "reserved" to the bishop, who alone could grant absolution, but that's not an issue. "I just give them absolution," he said.

He has met pro-abortion people "who see no problem at all" with it, are even willing to have an abortion "to be free for a vacation." For them "anything goes."

"I have not a lot of interest in their thinking," he said. Some of these "are worse than the real narrow pro-lifers." There are "so many levels."

To him "it's pretty obvious that destroying life in abortion is objectively evil." But at the same time, there are "many unanswered questions." His approach is that "anyone who has all the answers doesn't have a lot of wisdom. We all have little pieces of this puzzle."

Marriage and Divorce

As for divorce and remarriage, he has "questions about church marriage practices" but feels that as the church's representative, he should not bend rules in this matter.

When his brother, who had been a priest, wanted him to officiate at his wedding without authorization from the bishop, Mike declined. He did help find an Episcopal priest to officiate, however, and he preached at the wedding mass — a compromise that left everyone satisfied.

The only time he bent (broke) the rule in this area was when he recently married a couple in their seventies who did not qualify. The man, a Protestant, had been married several times. It would have taken "a couple annulments." The process would have been "very difficult," and the couple didn't have a lot of time.

"I am willing to perform the marriage and let God figure it out," he told them, but only if the woman's family, who were Catholic, would not find it "disturbing" and if a Catholic ceremony would not "cause more problems" than it solved. The woman decided it wouldn't, and the ceremony followed.

"A lot of times you want to perform the marriage," he said. But he holds back, again because of his official status in a legitimating organization, the church. The state recognizes the marriage he performs, assuming he is following his church's rules, he said.

Another reason is the public aspect of marriage, with banns announced beforehand. His is a small town, where people know each other's business. In a big city parish, where there is more anonymity, he would feel more comfortable "stretching things."

A Mixed Marriage Problem

A more common problem is raising kids Catholic in a mixed marriage. The Catholic party is supposed to sign a promise that the children will be so raised. Mike sees "a lot of hesitation, looking back and forth between the paper to be signed and the non-Catholic partner. A lot sign it who don't care one way or another. But where both are committed to parishes, as in our town, where there are a lot of Lutheran churches," he gives them an out.

"I say a strict interpretation says you raise the children Catholic. But it can also be read loosely, so you mean, 'I hope my children will follow in my faith.' I say it's something the two of them have to figure out. Not by leaving the kids alone to decide for themselves. That's no good.

"But if one is more involved in his or her parish than the other, I say it might be better if the kid is raised in that church, Catholic or not."

It doesn't bother him to marry a couple when the Catholic doesn't fully agree to the child-rearing requirement. His solution to the problem is something of his own devising, "based on practical need."

He feels that if these are "good people," it's not up to him to say they're not qualified. "They should be married in the Catholic Church," he said. "If we have to stretch things a little bit, okay."

Is it important to keep people in the church? He took the question as pertaining to defections to other denominations. "We do all we can to keep them," he said, referring to parishioners who join Pentecostal congregations.

But he has a disagreement with the other priests on the parish staff, who rate remaining Catholic higher than he does. "If parishioners find something elsewhere that makes them better people, I say let them go. Our church is good and worthwhile, but maybe it doesn't fit everybody."

He finds "great division" among priests on another question, the baptism of infants whose parents don't go to church.

At issue is whether "you test them, have them come ten weeks to church, make them jump through hoops" or "serve them where they're at, encourage them, not just tell them they don't measure up to our standards." He finds it "pretty hard to say no to somebody" and so generally baptizes the child, trying to make it clear to the parents that they are "taking on a commitment" without requiring extensive instruction or even mass attendance.

Altar Girls and Women

As for women's issues, he has "no problem" with women being ordained and "can't understand the people opposed to it." In his parish it's "not a big issue." The permanent deacon mentions it now and then in his sermons, to no response that Mike can observe. Neither is women's ordination an issue he wants to "invest a lot in." To him it "seems a lesser thing" than issues of racial justice or war and peace. "These," he said, "are more urgent matters."

Gays and Lesbians

Gay and lesbian problems do not loom big in the parish. At an interdenominational ministers' meeting, he spoke up as a minority voice against those, led by two black ministers, who called AIDS a heaven-sent punishment for gays. "I said AIDS sufferers are like lepers. You don't ask how lepers got it. We're supposed to be good to lepers, I told them. They didn't want to hear that."

Mike brought up the issue of gay priests. "My only problem with gay priests, guys I have known, is they tend to think that being gay they have some sort of permission to be sexually active and don't have the same obligation to respect their vows. I have tried to get an explanation from them, but I never could fully understand what they are thinking. Sexually active gay priests don't seem to feel they are violating their vows. It's a puzzlement to me."

He recognizes "the myth," that is, the general, unverified impression, "that lots of younger priests are gay, not only gay but openly and actively so." He paused. "The one or two gay guys I know, who have not been among the younger ones, have done very good ministry."

He combats homophobia. "I bring it up in school. I get giggles at first, then they settle down." This is in his white suburban situation. In an earlier assignment, he did the same at a black girls' high school, where he got the same initial reaction.

But after some discussion, one girl might say she had a cousin or friend who was gay or lesbian. "They started thinking then, realizing they knew gay people and shouldn't make fun of them. It's a real issue they have to deal with. It's good they hear about it."

Liturgy

Liturgically, another educational issue has arisen, whether to require confession before a child's first communion. "A lot" of pastors don't require it, he said, even though the rules call for early confession. At his parish, he and the director of religious education and the rest of the staff agreed it was better to wait until fifth or sixth grade for confession, where there is "more awareness of responsibility and guilt and all that — reasons we thought were substantial."

They went ahead and made confession optional before first communion, usually in second grade, leaving the "school program" about confession for later. But they were turned in. "One guy reported us to the chancery. We had a letter and a phone call, telling us we should prepare all the kids for early confession, making later confession the exception. We huddled again and decided if we were reported again, we would do something about it."

He considers the chancery in general "pretty good." He called about altar girls, another nominally forbidden practice, and was told, "Don't ask. Do what you think is right."

"Most down at the chancery have the sense to say, 'Don't ask for an official opinion, just figure out what to do.' I appreciate that. Ignorance is bliss sometimes."

In other liturgical practices, he considers himself not "real strict." For years in his parish, he and the staff have had worshipers at mass say the second half of the Eucharistic prayer with the priest. He first encountered it at an inner-city parish where many worshipers were Spanish speaking but the priests weren't. So the priest encouraged people to join in, to "help him along."

The practice is "probably reason for censure," Mike said. "But the phrasing fits." That is, the "we offer" words and the like apply equally to people and priest. "We feel real comfortable with it," he said, citing "common sense" as the deciding factor and adding as a fillip the joke about the liturgist and the terrorist.

"What's the difference?" he asked, and answered, "You can negotiate with a terrorist."

Another common liturgical adaptation is the communal penance service, what the priest in the first chapter was at such pains to keep hidden from the chancery. "We devised our own hybrid rite," said Mike. "We don't give common or general absolution. At Christmas time we have a service where each comes and mentions one or two faults to a priest standing in the front of church. The priest gives a word of peace, then when all have done that, we give absolution.

"It's not a full divulging of sinfulness. We're comfortable with that, and people seem to like it. My inclination in these things is that if it's for the good of the community and it means cutting corners, I'm inclined to do it."

The Pope

The pope? "I like the pope. People feel he's repressive in church matters but has a broad vision. I like his big picture of the Third World suffering because of a lot of things we do. We have obligations to them.

"One criticism with a ring of truth to it is that in what he has influence over, church stuff, he's very traditional, but in what he does not have influence, the world, he's progressive.

"But he's like a bishop, with not a lot of control over my day-to-day. The only worry is about his appointment of bishops. Very few progressive guys have been named. This will change the tone of the church. It's the one thing I'm scared of.

"Otherwise, his pronouncements or statements, I don't pay a lot of attention to. But he's a good guy. He's certainly spread a lot of good will around the world."

Liberal? Radical?

Where is he on the liberal-radical spectrum? "I'm not pro-law, but I have yet to think through my position on the law and the spirit.

"Charismatics, whom I've been dealing with for a long time, are great for using Paul saying law doesn't count, it has to be the spirit, law is negative and evil and all that. I like to quote back to them about fulfillment of the law, that some of the Gospels are pro-law.

"I tend to be in the middle. Law is for man, not the other way around. Laws are necessary and good, but don't make them absolutes. That's the only problem. If you crush people with the law, that's not good. But you can't just let the spirit flow.

"Still, the smorgasbord Catholic is not a real bad thing. The pope doesn't like picking and choosing, but that's the reality for all of us. When we moved the American flag out of church except for special occasions, like the Fourth of July, some very patriotic parishioners objected. In defense of what we did, we pulled out what the bishops said about limiting use of the flag in church. So we use what they say when we can't get a point across and ignore them when we want to do something different."

The Fantasy

What if everybody took the party line? "I don't know. One fact that goes against thinking the church will shrink is the experience of religious orders since the council. The most progressive orders have fared the worst in renewal. The more traditional have held on a little better.

"My fantasy says there would be fewer, more rigid people in the church. But something tells me maybe it wouldn't be that way."

Chapter 5

Fr. Bowen: A Lawyer Objects

FR. HENRY BOWEN, of Worcester, Massachusetts, objects to the title of this book. "I don't bend rules," he says indignantly, "I'm a lawyer."

He's a canon lawyer, a fourteen-year veteran of the diocesan marriage tribunal, thirty-seven years a priest, eleven years a pastor of St. Charles Borromeo parish, onetime president of the prestigious and progressive Canon Law Society of America. A progressive himself and proud of it, he is proud most of all, you gather from a lively conversation with him, of being a lawyer.

"The law protects rights. Are people who flout or denigrate the law carried away by the Spirit? Or by themselves, so they end up walking over people? You have to understand law," he said on the matter of law vs. spirit.

Moreover, in legal matters, he said, "I'm a Roman. According to the American philosophy of law, if a law is on the books, we must follow it. It's not so with church law. If a church law creates a grave burden disproportionate to its purpose, it falls of its own weight."

So don't talk about bending rules but about understanding law and applying it to protect rights.

As a lawyer, he has had a hand in bringing church practice around on several issues, including due process for priests and the annulment process.

Birth Control

The question never arises. People never ask. If they do, I give them the principles behind the prohibition: be generous, etc. I don't quibble with them. They make their own decision.

Abortion

It never comes up beforehand. If it did, I'd say "No way." If afterward, I try to be compassionate. I don't make them kneel in the snow in front of church. Again, it's very important to be careful here. They make the decision, not you.

Marriage and Divorce

Whatever you do, people have to take responsibility and know what they're doing. Twenty-five years ago, in my chancery office I took a call from a man in his second marriage, as was his wife, with thirteen children between them.

On advice of a priest, they were receiving communion without benefit of annulment. One of their thirteen kids had reached first-communion age, and a different priest, their pastor, had told him there would be no first communion for the youngster because of the parents' marital irregularity.

"Take your church and shove it," he told me. My complaint was less against the current pastor than with the original counselor, who had made the decision for the couple, who later couldn't stand on their own two feet.

It may have been a good decision to receive communion, even though it was irregular, but they didn't understand it. So when someone questioned it, they couldn't stand on their own feet. Their last state was worse than their first.

You can help people do this if the problem seems insoluble.

As a judge, I would issue a declaration of freedom to marry. As one sworn to uphold the law, in other words, I would appear to be bending it. But I wasn't.

Today it's a different situation, in that solutions are discoverable in most cases. The process is up to the challenge. It may take a year because of the clogged court load. But the first marriage took time, and so does this.

To take cases in order is the only fair way. For most you can find solutions, but for some there is no solution, and maybe there shouldn't be.

I was involved in developing the jurisprudence of Catholic annulment. It once was that one partner had to be proven balmy. Now the reason can be that even if they knew what they were doing, one or both were incapable — unable to make a go of marriage because of their emotional state. Civil jurisprudence regarding divorce was developing in the same direction at the time.

The Orthodox have their own approach to the marriage and divorce issue, by the way. Only the first marriage is sacramental. Then people are allowed two or three more non-sacramental marriages.

Today many decide for themselves on the communion matter. If as a pastor you see this happening, you don't raise the issue. If they bring it up, you talk to them. I'm a pastor, not a central investigation department.

Whatever happens, you take people where they are and try to move them along.

Altar Girls and Women

Altar girls are perfectly legal. The ban, once in footnotes, does not appear in the new 1983 Code. For that matter, the new law dropped the mass-server requirement completely. I've had altar girls since the new law, and so have my neighbors.

As for women priests, the ban is not of divine law but an old tradition that Vatican officials are loath to give up. It's not based on Scripture, I don't think.

Catholics will bend on this issue before the Orthodox do. Scholarship can get them over the God-given part. But Rome would still be reluctant because this change would distance it too far from the Orthodox.

Gays and Lesbians

Gays' and lesbians' orientation is innocent; its expression is immoral. But there's nothing wrong with their seeking companionship and affection. Again, I'm a pastor not a policeman.

Liturgy

Liturgically an issue might be choice of sponsors for a baptism — godfather and godmother. The law says they must be confirmed. But if they aren't, you don't kick them out. No, you start leading them along. Same with parents who don't go to church or have very little connection with the church. You start leading them along.

In the matter of general absolution, I see still some importance in individualizing the experience. So the people in this parish come up front with hands closed, and the priests open their hands as a symbol of being freed from their sins. When they have all done this and are back in their seats, the priests give general absolution. The ceremony combines the communal with the individual.

This is Rite Two of the code, requiring some action by the individual, rather than the stadium-full-of-people situation or soldiers massed before battle. In this situation the individual touch is important. So you use a sign given by each penitent, like the opening of hands.

The Pope

He's a hero to me. He's beautiful, doing a tremendous job. He's a tremendous presence and brings a lot of prestige to the church, traveling around. I don't agree with him, but he wouldn't agree with me either. His appointments of bishops are the problem. But even that can be exaggerated, because neither popes nor bishops have much effect on your day-to-day life as a priest.

Authority

Currently in the U.S., there are term limits for pastors. At one time I supported this, but now I prefer periodic review of a pastor's performance by his bishop, because the automatic removal puts you at risk.

As for troubles with my bishop and fear of retaliation, I have never had a problem. Nor have others I have known, including the priest who first used girl servers in this diocese. The bishop had him in twice, and he was picketed by the right wing, but he never bent. One priest screamed at his bishop when he was called in. One bishop moved priests every time he came for a visit.

The Fantasy

If priests in general went for the hard line, it would end the whole impetus of Vatican II. The world would pass us by and the church would fail to make change to meet modern times, which was the purpose of the council as I see it.

In Germany they thought they had a good church going, and along came Hitler, and they found they had no church there, as German Catholics went along with him.

In Holland before the changes, you bought a ticket for mass on Sunday. There were seven collections. When they took the wraps off, in a loosening up in the 1960s, the Dutch went extreme, like the nuns did when their restrictions were lifted.

Vatican II changes were to make the church relevant to our age. Thus Cardinal John Wright, once bishop of Worcester, was convinced at the council by the Polish bishops to go vernacular with the mass, because the mass was the only time priests could teach their people.

I still don't like your title.

Chapter 6

Fr. Larry and Fr. Bob:
Friends and Soul Mates of the '60s

FRS. LARRY ENFIELD AND BOB PINCKNEY are classmates and good friends from an ordination class of the late 1960s. Both are pastors in working-class suburbs of a major Midwestern city. Bob's work is heavily among "Latinos," including undocumented "illegals." Larry's is among white ethnics.

Bob grew up in a once-Irish neighborhood in the city. Larry lived and attended public high school in the shadow of steel mills. His parents had to be married in church before he could be ordained; it was something they had neglected for twenty-five years or so. His high-school homeroom teacher had put it to him: why not be a priest? She was "one of the significant reasons" he had become one. At a spry eighty-eight, she had shown up for his twenty-fifth anniversary.

We talked in a restaurant. Early in the interview, before the meal, Larry led us in prayer asking among other things that I be blessed and that my book "help many priests and lay people and the institution itself to see itself and be moved by the Spirit operating for good and wholesome change."

He also prayed for the waitress, by name, and for "those who have prepared this food plus our world, especially in the [just announced] peace accord between Israel and the Palestinians." It was all "through Christ our Lord, Amen." I was in business suit and tie; the two priests were in informal civvies. If the waitress noticed our praying, she never let on.

Bob said he saw this book as "practical theology, even Ecclesiology 101," using the term for theology of the church. The two of them gave me names of seminary professors who would recommend articles.

Birth Control

To the issues at hand, then. First, birth control. It rarely comes up, said Larry. "In the English world, no one mentions it," said Bob. "In the Spanish world, I'm the one who's pushing it." He laughed and continued: "I tell them this isn't Mexico, and you can't have twelve kids. I say that maybe after two or three you have to start thinking about birth control."

As for papal authority in the matter, Bob considers it a shame that the pope has wasted it on birth control. "It makes me angry, because papal authority can be very important. But people treat what he says about justice the same way they treat what he says about birth control. I find that frustrating."

In his basically Anglo community, Larry deals with people angry at the tension they have injected into their marriages by having five or six children because they felt obliged to do so. One family of nine suffers from having their mother "at church all the time and their father feeling victimized by this church law."

Among the Spanish-speaking, some young couples have the decks cleared in their consciences for having only two children. But if the choice is sterilization, it is often up to the woman, lest the man feel diminished by it, though it's quite a bit easier an operation for the man. "But it's not very macho," said Bob.

With regard to extramarital sex, Larry has been faced with the case of a young man who had the serious intent to engage in such behavior. Seeing his mind was made up, Larry told him, "Then you just better be protected, kid!" in reference to using a condom.

Bob recalled a "young Spanish guy" who died of AIDS, a father of four who had gone forth every Friday night to conquer more females, until he was stricken. Bob also recommends condoms to that type. He left safe-sex literature in the rear of church until reported to the chancery by "a Legion of Mary type." The regional vicar called and told him it was imprudent to leave it out that way.

Abortion

In Larry's parish is a woman who prays aloud every morning at mass for people in the right-to-life movement. He "clarifies" the issue now and then, "noting excesses" of the movement, always in the context of the "seamless garment" approach, which lumps abortion with capital punishment and other anti-life issues.

And discussing abortion, he is always "very gentle," careful of the guilt felt by women in the congregation—lower middle-class, ethnically diverse—who have had abortions. One woman with two babies and a husband in prison had back-alley abortions and was blaming herself for health problems ten years later.

The seamless garment ethic takes responsibility for the child in the womb and later. People ask him, and in essence he waffles, saying yes, it's a very serious matter, then, sometimes in the "pastoral mode I slip into," saying that is the decision the woman has to make. But he always encourages having the child and giving the child up for adoption.

Bob takes respect for life as "an ideal." He said, "We never get to the ideal. We must make decisions we can live with. I try to deal compassionately with those who come afterward. I say that's the idea we stand for."

A parish Bob served earlier had a clinic in the rectory basement "which stood for respect-life in all its forms," but if the physicians saw no alternative to abortions, they referred people to the university hospital. Only two of the thirty-seven physicians who volunteered were Catholic. "Many saw no problem with it and didn't even know why we hesitated," said Bob. In any event, he and the other staff permitted the practice.

Marriage and Divorce

When it comes to bad marriages, "We run our own chancery office," said Bob.

"All should be handled at the local parish level," said Larry. "If you want a priest involved who doesn't know you, go to another parish."

"We should get out of the marriage business," said Bob.

"Amen," said Larry.

"And administer the sacrament of matrimony only after ten years of marriage, giving the sacrament as a sign of what the couple has achieved," said Bob. It makes no sense "to bless eighteen-year-old love and hope it turns out well." But people with ten years together can say they have found a "life companion" in a relationship that is "a sign of God's love. Then it has meaning, and everybody in the parish knows it."

"We invite people to join the church," said Larry. "All these churches make announcements like this at this time of year. These people come, have some kind of conversion experience. Then we interview them and find they are in a second marriage and say you can't join until you get this annulment, which takes twelve to eighteen months and costs almost $1,000, not to mention digging up all that stuff" — what's needed to prove the first marriage was invalid.

"That is such nonsense. You say 'Welcome,' but then you put all those conditions on it. You say, 'You're not welcome, you can't even get into the program until your marriage is annulled.'

"Some do it, some say, 'Up yours.' Until a more compassionate approach is available, I must do the work of annulling. I've done that. I call my bishop here" — he turned to Bob, who chuckled — "and talk it over with him. He says, 'I think it should be granted.' It's a consultative process, showing respect for the tradition."

"I run into this all the time," said Bob. "Someone from a ranch in Mexico got someone pregnant when he was seventeen, was culturally forced into the marriage; it was a mistake, not a symbolic relationship. He has to pay $900 to have someone sign a paper?"

Mexican church authorities are not as concerned about records as U.S. authorities, he said. People must be married civilly there, and then by the church. "Frequently they do both, frequently neither."

Altar Girls and Women

Altar girls are fine in the Anglo community. Larry has used them for six or seven years. But Hispanic women do not like them. Mexican and from a very conservative tradition, they draw the line there, while doing a fine job leading prayer and Scripture study groups.

Larry tries to "raise consciousness" about sexism and the injustice of refusing ordination to women. He wrote about it in the parish bulletin, which someone copied to his bishop, who called him in on it. The bishop said it was too complex an issue for discussion in a Sunday bulletin and asked him not to do it any more.

Larry told him he disagreed. "We are a headline society," he told the bishop. "I want to create interest in the issue so that people want a more in-depth understanding of it. The bulletin can't do justice to the topic, but it can create interest."

They debated the issue itself briefly, never coming to agreement on it.

Larry substituted a communion service headed by women for a morning mass when the staff was cut back to just himself at the parish. These women, mostly "grandmother types," not college-educated and certainly not "radical feminists" such as some bishops rail against, give homilies at nursing home services too. Preparing for these homilies, they have ordered and studied sample homilies from one of the homily services.

Women ministers of care have asked him what they should do when they bring communion to a nursing home if someone of a different denomination wants to receive too. When they meet someone who hasn't been to confession in a long time, they ask, "Can we hear confessions?"

He has told them they should pray with the penitent for forgiveness and should give communion to the non-Catholic, urging the latter to see his or her own pastor at the first opportunity. "It is the church that brings Christ, not just the priest. The church is the mediator."

Liturgy

At funerals and weddings, Larry regularly invites everyone to receive communion. He asks that anyone who has been away from the practice of faith to make an "act of love and amendment of life," then to receive communion and at the "first opportunity make reconciliation with the church." He has gotten many back to the sacraments that way. "What a teaching moment, Jim!"

He noted that in the theology of the Eucharist itself there is forgiveness of sins and asks, "Why these add-ons? This control stuff? The Roman structure is one of control, not of empowering people so they can help themselves. It's one of 'We can turn the spigot on or turn it off.'

"Controlling your money is what it comes down to. When I say the church is not God, I say it's a vehicle that has come out of the historical Jesus in space and time. There is in it that kernel, that life force which is also very human.

"I respect my alcoholic, racist father. I love and respect him but I neither love nor respect a lot of what he does and says. So within that relationship, I can accept him for what he is but not all his teachings. In the same way, we should see canon law as corporate language, policies, and procedures."

They talked about having been seminarians in the 1960s. "One of the foundational events of our life, a profound influence," said Bob.

"Our revolution in consciousness began in the seminary, but it didn't really happen to me until I began my recovery from alcoholism, turning my life over to God daily, believing that God is the context in which I live and move and have my being."

"Ignatian spirituality," interjected Bob, referring to the principle in the *Spiritual Exercises* of finding God in all things.

"God is present in the event," said Larry. "Now what is the truth of the event? When we live in honesty, purity, unselfishness, and love, when we try to act humbly and try to do discernment of the Spirit with prayer, God is there for us. The church is not to be an impediment to this experience of God but a vehicle that allows it to happen. And Jim," he said, "it's not happening.

"Too much of external society is still with us. Younger priests are going back to externals. I know priests who do awful things on a personal plane, but conduct beautiful liturgies. It's not the sacraments they celebrate. We must be an institution of integrity. We must focus on spirituality, so that all our justice ministries grow out of our spirituality. We can't give what we don't have. What's that old Latin saying?"

He turned to Bob, who supplied it: "Nemo dat quod non habet," for "Nobody gives what he doesn't have."

"It's especially true with Hispanics," continued Bob. "Evangelicals have an impact on them because they give an experience of God. That's part of our tradition, to experience God."

The Pope

In past battles over authority, Larry has considered himself "a papist, an ultramontane," a supporter of papal infallibility. "But that man has to be in conversation," he said. When he comes to the U.S., for instance, "he doesn't talk to priests."

"Hispanic and Slovak people love the pope," said Bob. "They cherish pictures of him. I feel frustrated, because he's so likable but says such asinine things. But you can't talk too strongly against what he says, because the people love him."

Liberal? Radical?

On the liberal-radical spectrum, Larry chose "progressive" to classify himself. "In some things I'm very conservative, as in ethics. I consider there to be no advancement in the spiritual life without sexual purity and absolute rigorous honesty. Nor is there any in overcoming addictive behavior," he added.

"I'm very conservative in that but very tolerant and non-judgmental about people coming back in the conversion modality, and I'm very radical about justice. The church should be out there working for justice, and not on single issues. We should give people leadership training.

"We need laws. We need policies and procedures, as does any family: you lock the door, turn the lights out, flush the toilet."

"Any vibrant, living thing needs some order," said Bob.

Authority

They jumped into this one, emphasizing the sources of their attitudes, which they located first in the 1960s environment in which they were educated to be priests. "It colored our approach to law," said Larry, namely, the combination of being urged to move ahead but also to do as you were told.

For Larry this built on a "real distrust of authority" he had already imbibed as the son of an alcoholic father and "co-dependent" mother. He grew up never trusting his parents and later didn't trust authority in general. There were two pulls for him: one to trust authority, the other to trust "the person inside" him, who could see the mistakes that were "constantly" being made.

He loved his parents, even as he knew they were "out of it." He had to make that his conclusion, because otherwise why would they do what they did?

So in the seminary he was told the bell that woke him at 5:30 a.m. was "vox Dei," the voice of God in his life. The point was made but never explained. Larry never believed it.

"It didn't resonate with my own experience, my gut reaction. The whole business colored our whole approach to authority, for years afterward."

"Still does," said Bob.

At the same time Larry had the desire to be a "team player." He wrote about "the relationship" as the keystone of pastoral experience. Then he got out of seminary and discovered he was right. "Real strength is in the relationship, not in the laws."

Asked if there are some authors they depend on or recommend, Larry mentioned the gospel commentaries of Fr. Raymond Brown and Karl Rahner's *Spirituality for the Modern World.* "The vision he has," he said of Rahner, "the supernatural existential, how we are all built for God."

From others they have learned there is "always to be tension between the institution and the mission, the Petrine and Pauline elements." But "in pastoral ministry we must always come down on the side of the mission, at the same time bringing the Petrine institution along."

He likened it to balancing like the fiddler on the roof — always tradition, always change, a precarious arrangement.

"It's the function of the parish to call the whole cumbersome thing behind us to move," said Bob. "The thing is like a museum. It takes time for a painter to make it to a museum, and it takes time for a theologian to get there too. It's frightening.

We're not solipsists, creating our own reality. Rather, what we do is based in Scripture, congruent with experience.

"But if you get called down, your ass is in a sling, big time. On a little point, not canon law like marriage. They take it so seriously."

The Fantasy

What then if there was a universal hard line?

"I'm afraid that's going to happen," said Bob. "On some kind of forced issue: you have to believe this or else. I see numbers dropping, and no longer a celebration of life. I see the church as a big old curmudgeon, unable to enjoy life, totally irrelevant."

"I see a church of the self-righteous," said Larry, "an Opus Dei sort of church." He referred here to the semi-secret quasi-religious order founded in 1928 and believed to have grown mightily in influence under the present pope.

Opus Dei has "a lively outreach, appealing especially for people who need the rigidity of severe structures, who perhaps have no experience of God whom they trust and identify with. Truth and life is something external to them. They prefer a narrow-gate approach" to reaching heaven.

"But we have different backgrounds. What was it [he named the pastor of a parish near the seminary] told us when we went to help give instructions as seminarians?" He checked with Bob. " 'Eighty-five percent of the people out there are sick,' he said. That's why he had windows on the parlor doors. He didn't want to be closeted with people.

"Step back a bit, consider the numbers we are dealing with in ministry. None of us is from a perfect family. All have to come the narrow way to a sense of balance. We need guides and models and not just external obedience to rules but an inner grappling leading to personal realization.

"The church has to be a vehicle for this. There has to be creative tension between institution and mission. Priests are the ones who manipulate the symbols. We need the freedom to do that. If we come to the point where we are restricted, I hope it's not for nineteen years, when I will be old enough for my pension. I couldn't function in a church like that, and I wouldn't."

"Neither would I," said Bob. "I wouldn't feel authentic any more. It would be like an autopsy of the church. We would have taken the whole thing apart, understood it thoroughly, and killed it in the process. Everything would be in its place. We would have an intellectual feast day. But it would be a museum. It wouldn't be a church."

Chapter 7

Fr. Gardiner:
A Bow to the Majesty of the Law

F R. JOHN GARDINER is a city pastor with a ready smile and
an unbending view of the law, even as he bends rules. As
a young priest in the late 1960s in inner-city work, he once got
hustled out of a meeting by a black enforcer. He was in civvies,
and the young black man didn't like his looks. Caught in the
act of being shoved, the young Gardiner looked ready to give
as good as he got. Asked about it a few years later, he smiled
and said he had learned to realize that sort of situation meant
more to the young black guy than to him. He was learning, and
by now he has a huge plant to worry about and a large, highly
educated, racially diverse university congregation to serve. He
has come a long way from the church basement where he got
pushed around.

Birth Control

People make up their own minds. I ask a couple deciding when
to have children, "Why are you delaying that? Is it to achieve
material status or have a home? Is that self-centered, or an
honest concern? Are you waiting until you have your degree,
or a job?" They say they can't make that determination. I say
they have to. But I'm not the one to say their reasons are good
enough. The decision is theirs.

Abortion

Nobody asks about abortion either. Giving missions, I ask people what keeps them from feeling comfortable with God. If it's forgiven, I tell them, "Let it go, God wants you to be happy, as long as it doesn't mean being silly and is not at the expense of others."

In that situation people have said, "What prevents this is an abortion, years ago," or "It's my homosexuality." I'm not in a counseling situation then; so I accept this without comment and pray for peace and forgiveness and give absolution.

In the confessional on Saturday, four people come the whole afternoon, sometimes the same ones every week. Some come for counseling, but never to say, "I want to get an abortion." The church's position is clear. It's my position too, though I tend to wonder about rape and incest and the like. People don't ask me about that either.

The parish has a Respect Life committee, which is very good and tries to respect people. The parish has a number of medical people. If a "feminist for life" is speaking in town, the staff gets the word out.

In an earlier assignment, an inner-city parish, abortion was not seen as an option. It was not seen as a virtuous act at all, but as a shame when someone destroys her child.

Maybe we should talk about abortion more, but there's so much you can do in an eight-minute homily, except to admit this is not a clear issue. People tell me they really appreciate hearing there's room for discussion.

Marriage and Divorce

A woman came in who hadn't done the paperwork yet on her annulment and wanted me to schedule her wedding mass. I said I'd pencil it in, but she had to do the paperwork. Would I do the wedding at a hotel? I said no. Would I say the mass, have another priest do the wedding? That's confusing. She's trying for the semblance of a Catholic wedding.

Another pair wouldn't do the annulment procedure. Their first marriages were good marriages, they said. "We won't demean that by saying we didn't know what we were doing. We just wanted to know if you could do that." Marry them, that is.

I said I would love to do it. They were very close friends. But I can't get up in suit and tie, with or without the collar, and marry them, because it's totally against what the church is about. There is a way, and they didn't want to take it.

I sent them to a Lutheran minister. They went and were married and the next day received communion at our parish church. That's how they resolved it. I went to the reception wearing my collar. Hell, I wore it, because if I didn't, it would have looked like I was trying to hide something. They're my friends, married by a Lutheran priest. Let people think what they want. I wasn't going to skip the reception.

There's tension whether I like the couple or not. There are always people who say they don't want to go through the annulment process. Often enough they are not involved in the church, and that's part of the reason. I offer to help on paperwork. Then I feel unfair or disloyal, especially when a couple is trying to obey the law because one of them felt they had to.

The procedure is excruciating. A woman came in here who had just been through counseling. She wasn't sure about this process. I gave her questions she would be expected to answer, for her counselor to look over. If it's a moral impossibility, I told her, then according to canon law, she won't have to do it. The counselor said go ahead, and it was helpful for her. So the process isn't all bad, even if it is excruciating sometimes.

I think how you stand with church law is some indication of your relationship with God. It isn't everything, but part of it. A guy coming in for his third marriage wants to marry a Catholic. I tell him maybe he ought to get his life together.

It's different with someone struggling to work it out, when it's a matter of "Rome says no, you're on your conscience." Forgiveness starts with feeling guilty. The birth of a child makes you think of coming back to church. That's grace.

My approach is that the ministry is good news. On one side is the church structure with its rules, which I generally understand and appreciate. On the other is that pastoral sense: What do you say to a person? You go with what you have understood in terms of your own life and others' and the church without throwing the whole thing out the window.

I say, "I cannot answer this question for you about whether to marry again. I will give these guidelines, but you have to decide, either on worthy values or as a quick move to get out of this situation. I'm not the only authority. There are others who know you far better than I do."

I say, "You came to me to find out what the church teaches. I feel I should tell you that. It's a very strong word I am saying; it's a very strong authority. These are the foul lines, this to first base, this to third. Anything outside of that is definitely not the church's teaching. This is the operational area.

"Do you fit in there? I don't know. Are you a person earnestly seeking the will of God in all areas of your life, or are you habitually trying to cut corners?"

A couple came in, both married. Neither would be released by the spouse. Both wanted divorces. They were already in a relationship and asked what could be done. They started putting things out like "Don't you believe that if you're in a relationship and don't love one another, the best thing is to separate?"

I said, "I do, unless you're married. When you get married, you said you would do something different, that even if it wasn't working out, you were going to hang in there. You want me to say it's right what you're doing, but it's not right. By no standard is it right. Not by a civil standard, let alone by a personal moral standard. You want me to give you a blessing, then you can go on doing it. But adultery is dead wrong. I'm not bawling you out, I'm just saying adultery is wrong. Now the church has a way, an annulment procedure, where you can be in this relationship, but you have to get out of the previous one."

It was not a pleasant conversation. This guy was trying to get me to agree with him, and then they could go on. But it's adultery. Their relationship was being tested. For a number of reasons, the other partners wouldn't let them go.

They seek approval? As they sought absolution, which got to be seen as a sort of magic thing? Maybe. Some don't trust their consciences. I don't trust my own. But it's true, the decision by someone else is important. But laws sometimes seem in conflict with reality.

In a parish I was in earlier, a woman had married three or four times over twenty years, each time because she felt it was the moral thing to do. She wanted to marry again and faced a long process to undo this stuff. Her intended had been married three times. He didn't have her moral intensity; he would have gotten married in a minute. There was a question of baptizing him. The chancery said don't do it; it would validate an earlier marriage.

God, all these technicalities. "No, ways of getting to the truth," said the chancery. "Thanks for your advice," I said. It was insane. That case showed there was obviously something wrong here. We baptized him. There was nothing to be done about that long-ago marriage.

Another issue is what others will say. In a small town, everybody knows each other's business. But people come here from Los Angeles, and nobody knows they were married already. So where's the scandal? If one member of the parish starts going with another, that's different.

Another thing, living together before marriage. It's pretty obvious. They give just one address when they come to arrange the wedding. I ask, "What is your gift going to be? That is, what after marriage will be different for you two?" I raise the possibility of abstinence until marriage, saying, "Maybe it is to be your gift to one another, when you're married." It might keep them from taking everything for granted. I don't say it if they already have a kid. I don't tell them to move apart in that case.

A crazy thing: my cousin was in New York City this summer and heard a man talking about living with a woman. One priest wouldn't marry them, he said. They saw another who talked to them and changed their whole life. "I'll never forget Fr. Gardiner," he said. "That's my cousin," said my cousin.

I had put the couple through their paces, and it made an impression.

But all of that, premarital sex and the rest, people don't come and ask about it. And you can scare them away if you ask. But it's hard to ignore it. They know I know. One girl wanted their child baptized at their wedding. I said no, one sacrament is enough. They had the father of the bride carry the child into church.

Hey, it's pro-life! If I'd been asked, I might have said no, but it's best not to worry Father about that sort of thing.

There are some awfully good, spirit-filled people who stumbled somewhere, made a mistake, are really sorry. It would be helpful if we could say it's all right, but we can't always say that. We still say it sometimes. We tell people their relationship with God is all right.

Like intercommunion. It's wrong, absolutely. But what are you going to do in a mixed marriage, use separate churches? So the man goes to communion with his wife at her church. I know I'm giving communion to a non-Catholic spouse. Officially, you can never do that. But nobody with any sense would ever ask about it.

Altar Girls and Women

Pastoral authority is real. When I came here, this place had a liberal reputation. That was okay with me. I tend to think of myself as liberal. But people who weren't liberal came to see what I would do, expecting a change, like getting rid of the girl altar servers.

They asked, "Didn't the pope say such and such?" trying me out. "Yeah, he did," I'd say. "Then why girl servers?" they would ask. "Well, the pope wasn't thinking of the whole world. They got places where the church is spending all its time feeding starving people. Here it's different. The bishop wrote about it once and never repeated it. It was poor judgment on his part, and we priests told him so. When he comes here for mass, he will have girl servers, and he will not say a word about it."

"I don't know about that," was the reply. "Then write and ask him about it," I said. "Writing is the best thing you can do. The worst thing is for the bishop to believe everything is simple, and for him to think he will say something and everyone will go along. And I think it's a betrayal of trust to sneak around him."

In any event, I'm not for throwing out the law, or dismissing it as meaningless. You don't do that. Neither, like some, do you go with a literal interpretation. What you do is stay in the target area of what the law means. You hit the target. But you don't dismiss the law. I won't do it, because that destroys a lot of what gives stability to my ministry and my life.

I generally believe the law is a good thing. Some things in terms of liturgy I think are unrealistic. How can the pope travel around the world and think that Rome can make rules about what people can wear at the altar or who serves mass? It's inconceivable, given cultural differences. But the pope still insists he must be obeyed.

Take ordination of married men and women. Not marriage of priests. Parishes could use these people. My brother-in-law, who just died, a former priest, could have said mass while working as a public school teacher. He could have led Bible study and the rest.

I was asked to be on the diocesan vocations committee and said yes. We faced the problem: where were we going to find some single male celibates for this job? Run an ad in *Playboy*? There are some obvious solutions to this problem, but we can't talk about them.

Liturgy

Meanwhile, we hear about other stuff, like whether the priest receives communion first or last at a mass. We get a letter from the bishop about that. It's almost insane, how they worry about things like that.

I was one of the diocesan consultors at the time. The bishop was asking us whether he should write a letter on liturgy and obeying liturgical laws. Almost to a man, we said, "Don't do it. It would just cause more controversy. Leave it be."

I spoke up about the priest-communion thing. "You came out a month ago with this letter about a priest receiving first or last. We're going to hell in a handbasket. Who really cares?" I asked him. "I really meant that," he said. "Oh, never mind," I told him.

The Pope

The pope in Denver symbolized the institutional church but also my connectedness with people all over the world. My ministry is connected with that. I don't agree with all the rules, specifically about marriage. But the church has the right to say something about the conduct of our lives. And what it says has to be more than just opinion.

Liberal? Radical?

What influenced me, made me lean toward flexibility? Probably stuff I read, but I wouldn't say this book or this person changed my life. Mostly it's been people in day-to-day pastoral work who say this can't be right, there can be variations. In fact, certainty about some of these things makes me skeptical. If people would sometimes admit they are wrong, they would have more credibility. Like my bishop on girl servers. He said it was a mistake: he will never say another word about servers.

If conservatives allowed for the possibility they are wrong, would I be more inclined to believe them? Yeah, if they were just more human about the thing. But to say you can't even discuss this, that's crazy. What do you mean, you can't even discuss it? As if to say, "We'll not talk about sex in this house." Then where will we talk about it? The fact is, we *are* going to talk about it. It's like this is not a discussable issue. It's embarrassing, especially in a university community like this.

The problem is to know where to make exceptions to the law, how to define the target area, where to call on my pastoral authority. That's a hard one. A friend asks me to do one thing, my position calls on me to do another. Friends leaving the priesthood, for instance, ask me to do their unauthorized weddings. I can't do that.

Still, it's one thing to say this is policy. But there may come occasions when there's a gap in the rule, which doesn't cover every possible circumstance. *Epikeia.* The intent of the rule is to help people, not to screw them up. I *hope* that's the intent. It would be great to think it's all coming out of the same reasoning used when they search you on entering a plane. "Frustrating," my mother says. "Mom," I say, "they're protecting us."

Same with the law: Rome just wants to make sure we're all right. But you don't get that feeling. Sometimes it's just a display of power, and the more it's displayed, the more unreasonable it can seem.

Authority

I don't like the "bending rules" idea. I prefer to speak of "by what authority?" I say, by pastoral authority, as when people challenge me on using inclusive language at mass. But that's minor stuff. Generally I obey the law. Sometimes I make exceptions, but I don't go by the seat of my pants or by my feelings.

I'm not impressed by people who feel above the law. "What Jesus would do" is usually what I feel like doing myself. It's not my approach. The meaning of my ministry is not doing my thing, but being part of a much larger thing.

I recognize authority. I recognized Smith's authority [name changed: reference is to a notoriously unpopular bishop whom Gardiner tangled with publicly]. That's why I fought with him. It was wrong on both sides. Naylor [name changed: an auxiliary bishop] took me out to supper, to a very nice restaurant. That told me, "Hey, there is a bishop who's worried about you."

Matt Newberry [name changed: a widely respected veteran pastor keeping as low a profile as possible in those days] asked if I was planning to leave the priesthood. I said I wasn't, though I was considering leaving the diocese.

"Okay," he told me, "because if you were to leave the priesthood over money, women, or drink, people would understand, but if you say you're leaving because of your bishop, people won't know what you're talking about."

I appreciate the permanence of the institutional church. If I can do so much and no more, it's worthwhile, because I don't have to finish it. Someone else can finish it. In a sense, the church is my security. What kind of life could I get into that is so much connected, so worthwhile? Many of those who left the ministry went into fields equally significant, but it won't continue beyond their lifetimes. There's no one to pick up where they leave off.

Chapter 8

Fr. Hawkins Spills His Guts

F R. DONALD HAWKINS has two decades of ministry behind him and now heads a city parish in a lively, polyglot neighborhood. One of its Sunday masses is in Spanish. A busy man, he talked on the telephone, urging an on-the-spot interview if I wanted a "juicy one." Harassed and depressed, he was looking for an outlet.

Birth Control

Birth control has not come up in ten years, in the confessional or anywhere else. The church has spoken, and the church is the people of God.

Abortion

People don't ask, but some come to me in their struggle. After six years as pastor, people feel they can talk to me. Some say they are going to have an abortion; some say they are not going to have one. But no one comes to ask what to do. All come to know that the church still loves them, no matter the direction they take.

I tell them that. I say, "I'm not a judge and I'm not a jury. You must do what's in your heart. This is not cheap grace, not an easy answer, but a tough answer, because you have to decide what you are doing and why."

I also work with a local program that provides a positive, nonjudgmental alternative. It tells the woman, "If you choose to have the baby, we're with you," be it in Lamaze natural child-birth training, a new-moms discussion group, a grandmothers group, even a group that meets on the birth date of the aborted fetus. It also deals with birth control, which is controversial, and does a lot of education in high schools and other groups.

Marriage and Divorce

Our parish has a lot of young people, and I run into bad marriages quite often. I have a number of annulment cases pending, and I have invoked *epikeia* in my office, once for a couple who had begun the annulment process in another parish. The wife had been beaten almost to death by her former husband, and it was crucial that he not know her whereabouts. She was in counseling. As she started to fill out the questionnaire, horrid memories returned. Her counselor said the process was doing harm. I put the process aside and offered to marry them. But I explained what I was doing and made it clear it was up to them.

It's also very common for me to tell divorced and remarried people it's okay to come back to communion.

Altar Girls and Women

Women's ordination is becoming an issue as I try to educate people on the priest shortage. We basically are a sacramental church but are crucifying it on the cross of a male celibate priest-hood, claiming it's more important than sacraments. I raise the issue more at meetings than from the pulpit, which is more for homilies.

Gays and Lesbians

It's a growing issue in this neighborhood. I have met with and counseled gay and lesbian parishioners. Their being gay or lesbian has had no effect on their involvement in parish life. For instance, some have posted names of their HIV-positive partners on a prayer wheel in the back of church, where others sign up to pray for them.

Liturgy

I employ unauthorized innovations if they bring people closer to God in prayer. For example, we do not have baptisms at mass because they bring attendance down. The only parents' prayer is, "Please God, let mine be the baby not crying." Instead, we do baptisms individually, with as many as sixty relatives and friends on hand with cameras and the rest. Parents and godparents are prepared in groups led by parishioners. We put baby pictures on the baptistry wall.

The Pope

He's a teacher, and I listen to him and adapt what he says for our situation. I am not disloyal to him, because of my theology of what a pope is. He has yet to speak infallibly.

But people experience the church in the parish. They want a church they are at home in. If we can educate them to seeing the church as more than a congregation, that's good. But we start that process in an open church, not in a highly structured one.

I don't believe the man understands the American church. We Americans dissent and remain loyal. We have an election every four years without a revolution. He thinks questioning is disloyal, but it isn't.

He should realize this is the most loyal church he has. It contributes more and has the highest attendance. He calls us disloyal because we will not accept everything without questioning. But we are not an immigrant church any more. We question everything.

A bigger problem is with the bishops. He is appointing extremely cautious men, each thinking how he can rise farther. They are not a pastoral group.

Liberal-Radical Argument

I'm not crazy about labels. Does liberal mean you're open to new ideas? Fine. I see myself as a pastor. If it means liberal or radical in some situations, I'm radical. The gospel is a radical message. If it means challenging people of a conservative stance, fine. When I see needs, I respond. Unfortunately, when I do that, people class me as radical, which is scary.

Authority (and a Cry from the Heart)

If you asked me twenty-four hours ago if I fear retaliation, I would have said no. Now I'm not so sure. Some things are coming down the pike that scare me. I've written things and taken a leadership role. The bishop has come and we have discussed it. I've been honest and haven't hid from anybody. How long I can do that, I don't know. There are so many ways they can catch you out there. Some of it's happening.

The whole pederasty thing. A simple accusation can destroy a person. The minute a priest is accused, it's over. There is no way people trust you after that. The media will destroy you. What's in a priest's files, nobody knows. Even anonymous accusations are reported back to priests, who are left hanging.

It will get worse. The media have done a terrible disservice. The church covering it up did a disservice. The church is playing catchup now, but in the process some are going to be hurt badly.

Other things can happen. Financial: they can cut your grant. You get a reputation as a troublesome priest. You get called in for little things. Your next assignment is not as a pastor. It happened to one priest who for good reasons left a parish after six months as pastor.

It's an extremely political church, extremely fractured. There are people who feel they are right and can do anything they want. They have a sense of fundamentalistic morality.

Among priests there is profound distrust of the leadership. The bishop is a good man, but people around him are a problem. He's not a good administrator. In other dioceses it's worse. You feel very alone and very vulnerable. Preaching, you don't know who's going to write a letter.

The vicar called me about a complaint by a woman who said I wouldn't baptize her two children. "What's the problem?" he asked. The problem was the parents weren't Catholic and weren't willing to take instructions to become Catholic. But he asked, "What's the problem?" He doesn't call about the good job you're doing.

We priests don't support each other. We're solo operators. We gossip about each other and put each other down. There's an almost unhealthy glee in others' problems. There's no attempt to bring ourselves together.

If you had asked me two years ago to take a leadership role and I knew then what I know now, I would not do it. It's tearing me apart. People come and talk to me confidentially about things, but there's nothing I can do. I've been very devil-may-care. People said, Be cautious. I laughed. There are land mines out there, they said.

Am I another paranoid priest? I sound that way. But I happen to love what I'm doing. And to think that could be taken away....

The people respond beautifully. Being a pastor is tough, but being a good pastor is easy, I say. People respond here in the parish, but I'm part of a larger church.

It's when I move out of the parish that I wonder if it's worth it. Some priests stay in the parish. But part of me says you have to care about the whole church. This is a malady, that priests say they are busy in a parish and haven't time for the rest.

In the '40s and '50s in this diocese, people in my age group were putting together diocesan and churchwide initiatives. But you need creative juices for that, and now priests' energies are absorbed in their parishes.

The Fantasy

If pastors held to a hard line, we would be protecting empty buildings. An American Catholic schism could happen. Pressures are building. Something has to give. Or has it already given? Are we putting bandages on gaping wounds? The people of God are telling us we are not discussing the issues, which are a clergy that's open to everybody — men, women, married or not — and a church that is not passing judgment on people's lives.

We can't keep closing parishes. Every time we meet, it's about how to deal with losses. No one wants to deal with the issues, like women priests and married clergy.

Are we heading for doing six weddings at once? I was not ordained to go to six churches on a Sunday to say mass, say the magic words, and pour the magic waters. I'm more than a sacrament machine.

Do I want to be a Graham Greene priest ["the whisky priest with a bastard child" on the run from the government in Greene's novel *The Power and the Glory*]? No. Look what it did to him. We are not a healthy lot. We're killing ourselves.

We don't read. Look at a priest's shelf. Some go out with the same guys every Wednesday for twenty years. Their world has gotten very small. We don't take care of ourselves. We will shrink as a species all the more quickly.

One thing more. We have to be open to the power of the Spirit. We are just a blip in history. The Holy Spirit is guiding us and will take us somewhere. That's what keeps us doing the job we do. It's keeping the dream alive.

Two years ago my best friend, a priest, died of AIDS. We worked it out in his last days. He wanted me to say he had AIDS. I did so in his funeral sermon and got 150 letters from people pouring their hearts out, at least two-thirds of them clergy.

It wasn't just the AIDS reference. People mentioned everything under the sun. They wrote because they thought they had found a compassionate ear. I didn't want to hear it. I was just a friend taking care of a friend.

Chapter 9

Fr. Isham: A Seasoned Perspective

F R. STAN ISHAM heads a large city parish with a high gay
and lesbian representation. Ordained more than forty years
ago, he is one of the oldest priests interviewed for this book.
He deprecates his "simple Simon theology" but shows himself
well-read and thoughtful and ranges beyond the set questions.
It seemed good to let him range.

Birth Control

I would love it if the pope gave his position on birth control
as an ideal that in some circumstances is morally impossible.
People can't be held to a moral impossibility. My sister died at
forty-nine, right after giving birth to her seventh child. It was
a surprise baby. She had done her Christian duty. People are
bitter from that era.

A no-birth-control society is ideal in a wonderful world,
living on the farm with ten kids and so on. But what of the
population explosion and the concentration in big cities?

The naivete of the priesthood! I look back on the advice I
gave married couples forty years ago. I followed the rules and
explained them to people, like a nice kid of fourteen or sixteen who worked hard and knew nothing. The groom would
come to me the night before his wedding, to ask about how
not to hurt his bride. Both were virginal and knew nothing. I
was twenty-six and knew nothing either. The whole society was
that way.

Priests got no training as counselors. The vast majority realized this and took courses on their own, as I did.

Abortion

Should we forbid abortion after a trimester? After conception? The solution may be arbitrary. Our public policy should be to follow the wisdom of the people, who overwhelmingly reject abortion on demand as birth control. But after incest or rape? Another story.

The pro-life people go too far. They have an unprovable thesis, which is the safest, namely, that conception is the point where life begins.

Marriage and Divorce

In dealing with second marriages, I return to the moral-impossibility factor. Should I tell them to break up their marriage? In confession I tell them, "Say your regrets. Do the best you can." I can't do anything for it externally.

These are sincere people, who love the church. I can see why the church says in internal forum, "You're okay, but we can't do anything." So many just want to receive communion, while many others who can receive it don't care about it.

Imperfect Contrition

Even in the strictest theology, if you're truly sorry, you're forgiven. There is no distinction any more between perfect contrition (entirely for love of God) and imperfect contrition (partly for fear of punishment). All contrition is imperfect.

As a young priest in a parish with fifteen nursing homes, I would go around giving last rites to patients before I went on vacation, so they would go to heaven if they died while I was gone. I didn't trust them to have perfect contrition, which sent them to heaven anointed or not.

We were taught rigorism as seminarians so we wouldn't be "laxist," too loose in our moral judgments and preaching. Priests worked hard for nothing, living an ordered rectory life that was sometimes very pleasant, sometimes very bad.

Young Priests Today

Some young priests today think the world began in 1965. They have no perspective. They don't feel part of the universal church or have love and reverence for it.

Some attend wide-open seminaries and never learn to use solitude, to be creative with their time, to read and think. They don't study the classics or philosophy or history or logic. Arguing with them, it's always "I feel this way" or *ad hominem* arguments.

But you can't be a leader in the church or anywhere else without the classics and an introduction to the arts as well. Psychology, which they get, deals with the abnormal. It is literature that gives insight to human nature — that and history, music, and dance.

Most have no experience of liturgical music. One young priest, on hearing Gregorian music, said he didn't know such music existed.

Altar Girls and Women

We have altar girls but say nothing of it. When the bishop comes, we have no altar girls. Last time, we forgot, but he didn't care.

Vigilantes? There's the conservative *Wanderer* crowd. But I spend much more time on liberals. They can be just mean. Name-callers, some with authority problems from their father. Extreme feminists — "femi-Nazis," says Rush Limbaugh — who give genuine feminists a bad name.

I laugh at Limbaugh. I read the counter-feminist Camille La Paglia, with her statements like "Men are dangerous beasts" from whom women need protection. World consciousness is changing. We are just starting to realize it.

Feminists in the church have not quite figured out their position. A woman theologian talked here about women's ordination, which she favors. She noted there were no women bishops in the earliest years, though women were strong church leaders at the time. But the Holy Spirit may be saying now is the time.

Women's leadership has been wonderful here. Our parish council presidents have all been women. The current president, a feisty Filipino woman, is not made to feel guilty by Hispanics asking why we have no Hispanic priest. She tells them, "Find me one!"

There is much untapped leadership among women. I see a woman eventually as parish leader and presider at liturgy though she is neither pastor nor priest.

Gays and Lesbians

The gay-and-lesbian cause took us by surprise. We should not be self-flagellant about our reaction or even our recent record. If it came as a surprise to the church, so was it a surprise to society as a whole. This and similar issues have come to the fore only in the last twenty-five years.

A few years ago, we took homosexual behavior as a perversity. Then some sensitive writers and others raised our awareness.

The church saw it as a threat to marriage and family, because when everyone was married, it meant marital infidelity. There was no gay society in which gay couples could function. Even today, in the Latino culture there is no gay society. You have to be married. But the same percentage of them are gay. So the gay Latino becomes an adulterer.

Only in the last twenty-five to thirty years has this society arisen, and with it the practice of neither marrying nor taking a vow of celibacy but openly living as gay. In this new light, there can be a beautiful relationship between two men or two women. And this relationship can be the moral best a person can do.

I don't blame anyone for not understanding this. If I were a father, I'd be disappointed if one of my children didn't get married and have kids. But for most in our culture it's a moral impossibility not to be involved sexually, gays included.

I deal with activists and agitators on the point. They have no patience, and I find that understandable.

Liturgy

Most liturgy is not working, partly because of priests' ignorance. Some make it up as they go, but I don't know a priest who is gifted enough to do that. Liturgy should follow the book, which gives options. Public liturgy needs order and control. The larger the group, the more need for order.

One priest recently said a wedding mass with his back to the people, not wanting to be separated from the couple by the altar! He turned around with host and chalice at the consecration, thus achieving greater intimacy, he said. But he looked like a clown.

It isn't new. The Latin rite was massacred too, with fifteen-minute masses and the like. Too many today grandstand, wanting to be the star of the liturgy. But people in this neighborhood want what bespeaks otherness, the mysterium. It is beyond, it's mystery.

A number of young people are attracted by the liturgy here — our fine choir, our two organs, our good music both ancient and modern.

Not for a minute would I return to the Tridentine mass. But reformers changing the language may have missed the point. Sometimes it's better when you don't know what it means. We enjoy opera, don't we?

Sermons are another problem. A lot of priests are not trained to prepare sermons. It's an insult to think you can just get up there and talk. On vacation in small Wisconsin towns, in the forced intimacy of country churches, I sit in the congregation. One day I did the unthinkable: I walked out on a bad sermon. I drove to a nearby Episcopal church, where I sat in back to hear the sermon.

The Pope

I believe most firmly in the Petrine ministry, and I'm upset that the pope is alienated from the church over a few issues. I see no need for a change in structure, though maybe in the pope's manner of governing. He is one of the great political popes.

Why he hasn't called back married priests, I don't know. He's in love with the Orthodox, who have them. It would solve the priest shortage, if just for Sundays, when parishioner-priests could preside over the Eucharist. People would not be scandalized.

Not as they are by pedophilia cases. Most feel like vomiting. Still, the people have handled it very well. Priests do a bad imaging of themselves, but people don't seem to apply it to them, as when they hear of doctors charging too much and reply, "Not my doctor." Through it all, attendance has been up.

Authority

As pastor I tell the parish council I can go against what they want but I would be a damn fool to do so. Still, the pastor has to be creative and offer a vision and some magic. He stamps his personality on a parish. It's okay as long as it's an acceptable personality. It's a coalition, pastor and parish leaders. The pastor is not the only leader and not the only one with a vision. This means consultation, though sometimes there is too much consultation. This diocese is a stagnant pool of it.

Parishes should specialize. One parish near this one is where ex-religious can meet and vent their anger, another is a warm family place full of kids. This place follows my interests, with our prayer center, for instance, which teaches how to pray and meditate. We have high liturgy and good music. People come here for that.

Some who live in our boundaries go to other parishes. We even send them elsewhere when we know that's what they are looking for. One place can't do it all. Parishes are not competitive but complementary.

It all circles around the pastor, who has a vision and is supposed to help the laity accept that vision and preserve what they want of it when he's gone.

I say such wise things, talking to you, but day to day I make a lot of mistakes.

This parish has quite a mix: rich, poor, gays, Hispanics, and others. It's a juggling act to get some semblance of unity. The pastor must be unprejudiced, open to all sorts. Rigidity is one of the things that could go wrong.

We have parish rules based on how few priests are here — only two for three thousand families, with eight masses on a weekend. You can't become a mass machine, it destroys you. So you have rules and regulations for self-preservation — no Sunday weddings, for instance. You explain it, but people aren't happy.

We permit no weddings or funerals of people from outside the parish. You went here to grade school? Where do you go to church now? It's hard to say no; they can guilt you like crazy.

Or music for wedding masses. You say, "That music is more for the reception." You try not to be arbitrary. People say, "It's my wedding. Why not have what I want?"

But I have seen no rigorism. In group absolution, where there are so many penitents you can't handle them individually, you apply rule two [from canon law, one of three options]. When we do something out of the ordinary, we blow no horns. You do the best you can, but make no crusades out of incidentals, putting the bishop on the spot, embarrassing him.

The Fantasy

The hard line would lead to a tiny church. The vast majority want to go to church and be close to Jesus and pay no attention to church disputes. As for myself, it's been my destiny to be a priest, and it couldn't have worked out any better. I couldn't have been a natural father. I would have been unsatisfied with my children because they weren't perfect.

Chapter 10

Fr. Innsbrook: The Bottom Line

F R. RONALD INNSBROOK heads a thriving parish in an old, renovated neighborhood in a Midwestern city. The parish is "middle class at most," with 480 families — 40 percent from outside parish boundaries, drawn, he says, by its "warmth and sense of freedom."

More than forty years a priest and fourteen years pastor of this parish, he relies heavily on a priests' support group that has met weekly for sixteen years. During their two-hour meeting, the priests — once fifteen of them, now only six — "share and reflect on Scriptures." They tell what's bothering them, let their anger out, discuss their plans.

Four have talked out their plans to leave the ministry and have done so with the group's blessing. One of the group might kneel in front of the others, who pray over him, whatever his situation. Fr. Innsbrook derives great comfort from these meetings.

Before he was a pastor, he taught high school and then seminary students. Now sixty-nine, he expects to retire soon. His is a richly anecdotal set of responses.

Birth Control

From the pulpit I say nothing about birth control. It's no place for it. I haven't been asked about it for I don't know how long. People are handling it in their own way.

Abortion

Women come after their abortions, dealing with guilt feelings. Even men come whose young ladies had an abortion they were responsible for, feeling their guilt, sometimes years later, wondering if God will ever forgive them. The problem seems to be they haven't forgiven themselves. I tell them that. It seems to touch a chord.

Beforehand, they don't come around. Oh, one came a year or so ago and decided to put the child up for adoption. I'm on the board of a group that provides help and counseling. A couple started it, former parishioners of mine, not the diocese. Now the group has four houses where women can stay, with doctors on call.

Marriage and Divorce

I send very few cases to the tribunal. I feel I know as much as the tribunal knows. With simple cases, I say, just go to confession. Some hesitate and have to pray about it.

I noticed one lady in her second marriage was not going to communion and asked her about it. She said her request for annulment had been denied. I said if they refused, she was a natural for internal forum. Now she's a daily communicant, and her husband is back at the table too. Then her ex-husband called and came to see me, and I told him the same thing. He decided, "Why not?" and now he's back at the table too.

Altar Girls and Women

I don't ask the bishop about girl servers and the like. I know what the answer would be. He objects to girl servers, but when he came for confirmation, I had them on the altar, and he said nothing. If the girls are faithful at it, why not?

Visitors say, "You have girl servers?" I say I didn't notice. "But the pope said you're not supposed to have them." I say, "Is it logical for him to say that?" "He's the pope." "But he allows women to be Eucharistic ministers, which is more important than lighting candles," I tell them.

I see no logical explanation for the prohibition. It reminds me of the saying, "Hey, wait for me, I'm your leader." The pope will one day say, "Yes, you can have altar girls."

As for women in general, one reason I helped bring the deacon program to this diocese was to get people used to a married minister. No women deacons have been ordained, but women are doing a lot of good things. In time there will be women priests, but I probably won't live to see it.

Sometimes we have women preaching. I start off homily time with a few sentences, then I say that I'm going to share this pulpit with Sister So-and-So, or the pastoral assistant, who might be a woman with six kids.

Gays and Lesbians

Our neighborhood is a kind of settlement for gay people. This created some problems. Some of our Catholics moved out when gay couples moved in. I had been kind of fed up when I was teaching at the seminary, seeing so many gay people going on to the priesthood. Then I came here and found them all around me. I had to get in touch with my sexuality, so as not to scare them or let them scare me.

I have blessed homes of gay people. When someone gay calls from outside the parish to go to confession, I ask why. "Someone in the community said you would be kind and open to me," is the answer. It's been a non-judgmental role for me. I don't accuse them of anything.

At the same time, it's a little scary the number of gays being ordained. A gay priest told me that of his class of ten, all were gay — two in the closet, the rest out one way or another. This was ten or eleven years ago. Some have left the ministry in the meantime. "All?" I asked the man. "All," he said.

Liturgy

The four churches of my vicariate have been very cooperative in coordinating reconciliation services, and we have almost always had enough priests for individual confession. I have given general absolution only once.

The Pope

I feel sorry for the pope. It's an overwhelming job, and he is not able to bend much. I pray for him. Even being a bishop these days is difficult.

Liberal? Radical?

My being liberal or radical depends on the issue, on the compassion I feel, on what moves me to take a stand.

Authority

In general, I'm not much for titles. The bishop made me a monsignor over my objections and knowing that thirty years ago in the priests' senate we asked that there be no more monsignors. Four bishops went along with that until this one. I told this one that in conscience I couldn't come to the ceremony. He sent me a fancy paper from the pope.

I took some flak from some other priests who thought I was being falsely humble. I said I'm not into that, it's not what the church is about.

It was disruptive for him to do that. I told him there would be a lot of hurts from what he had done. I was living with a retired priest and asked, Why me and not him for some kind of rank?

I asked people not to call me monsignor and told them I would change neither my attire nor my attitude. I am "Fr. Ronald," cordially, and remain that. I will never use the title or wear the crazy robes. Correspondence from the bishop's office comes to me as "Monsignor." It angers me.

The bishop told me, "I'm not giving this just to my friends." A parishioner, a former student of mine, said, "If he had not given it to you, he would have heard from us. He gives it to you, and he hears from you."

The bishop knows I differ with him. As chair of the personnel board, I opposed a number of things. I have felt I am serving Christ. My allegiance is to the Lord and not to any human being. A vow of obedience had to be taken at the time of ordination.

But it's certainly a conscience matter, and if the Lord is asking me to do something differently, I have to respond to that.

I had an interesting experience in 1986. We were trying to renovate this church, to update it to meet modern needs, especially in our worshiping environment. I had discussed this with the diocese's director of liturgy and had been reading the bishops' guidelines for such a renovation. Then I started preparing the people for the change.

My predecessor here, a former seminary rector, had done nothing. He never walked in the back of church after mass. He talked to people only through the confessional grille. He appointed no Eucharistic ministers, because some parishioners were opposed to it. I had to renovate the people before the building. I was eight years or so bringing them along.

Finally, we were ready. I was going to move the tabernacle closer to the people, taking it out of the sanctuary. A railing was to be put up in the back of church, with a sign saying, "As you pass this, you are in the sanctuary." It told people there was no barrier between them and the priest, that they were praying with him.

Meanwhile, a millionaire parishioner who had controlled my predecessor called the bishop and offered to give the parish a million dollars if I did no more than a paint job. The bishop called and asked me what I was doing. I told him, including about how the changes followed the bishops' guidelines. He told me of the woman's offer, dependent on our leaving the tabernacle and altar rail in place.

I told him if he wanted that, he should find himself another pastor. No way would I let one person control a parish. "How much would it take for the next person?" I asked the bishop. He pulled back. "Okay, I understand," he said.

The woman switched to another parish, which got all the bucks when she died.

This is what I had to do. If the bishop was going this way, I had to tell him not to count me in.

Chapter 11

Fr. Logan: An Old Europe Hand

F R. CHARLES LOGAN has been a priest for thirty-plus years, about half that time as a pastor in a Midwestern diocese. As a young priest educated in Europe and speaking three languages, he attended a session of the Second Vatican Council, acting as a secretary, passing out documents and the like.

Later he headed the "presbyterate," or priests' senate, of his diocese, an elective position. He has been a teacher and held other appointive positions in the diocese. He gave a good deal of thought to discussing these matters, asking and getting several weeks to think them over.

Birth Control

Paul VI, a very conscientious, almost scrupulous person, feared the demise of natural law, and so he rejected two groups' advice and reaffirmed the birth control prohibition in 1968. He was heavily influenced by Cardinal Alfredo Ottaviani [a strongly conservative papal aide], and he rejected both groups.

It was the beginning of change among Catholics regarding fidelity to the church's line, as Andrew Greeley has reported. It remains the scandal *par excellence,* with the present pope repeating the prohibition — it's absolutely wrong, he says — in Latin America and most recently in Denver. To lay that on poor people in Latin America contributes to a breakdown in moral teaching.

I didn't teach it. In confession I would hear people out and be understanding. If pressed, I would tell them not to be too hard on themselves, because moral theologians say it's a matter of conscience, which is what the Canadian bishops said at the time, even with papal teaching as strong as it was. McCormick and Curran are right [Richard A. McCormick and Charles Curran, both moral theologians who have taken issue with the absolute prohibition].

For commentary on this issue, I like *America* magazine best of all. In a recent reference to Cardinal Suenens's memoirs [a Belgian, considered a progressive during Vatican II], Paul VI comes off as a scrupulous person. So the flock was led by someone who had his own problems to contend with?

The key issue is, do we have absolutes? Or can everything be demythologized? I don't think people are going to follow the absolutes position, including priests. Are we culturally conditioned to do so?

Abortion

Abortion is more complex than birth control. More is concerned here. Birth control is almost passé, but abortion is still on the front burner. Extremists complicate the issue. I am opposed to abortion and have preached against it, but I wouldn't picket. Beyond that, I'm not sure what to say.

Medical discoveries will change the question, making it even more complex. If asked, I would always say abortion is wrong, but never in a way that lays guilt on people who have been involved in one.

Marriage and Divorce

I run into many, many bad marriages. I never turn anyone away. Even now, with annulments more available, people take it into their own hands — though maybe not with a big church wedding for the second marriage. But the twice-married become involved in church, even in their own parishes. The pastor may even invite them to become involved in ministry, sometimes without knowing their situation.

More internal forum is used. Once it was mentioned only in Richard McBrien's book *Catholicism*. Now it's common. Most people are apathetic on the issue, because church is not important to them. It's the conscientious ones who go through the process or seek out a priest in internal forum. Most just go back to church, married twice or not, sometimes after waiting for a change of pastor.

Altar Girls and Women

In this diocese one out of every four parishes has altar girls. In my last parish, I was for having them, and people were asking about it, but our deacons voted it down.

Gays and Lesbians

I tried being empathetic with a gay man who came to me ten years or so back, but it backfired. The man, a bartender, got angry about it. He was expecting me to condemn gay behavior, maybe hoping for a conversion.

But I haven't been approached much. A priest friend of mine says my lack of empathy comes through, and that's why they don't come to me, though my reading has made me more tolerant. I try to be honest from the pulpit, and my feelings must come through.

Liturgy

I've changed words in mass prayers and used a crystal chalice, though you're supposed to use a metal one. For a time I said "peoplekind" rather than "mankind." Now I just say "people." For years I encouraged people to hold hands at the Our Father. It helps to build community. And also for years I have passed around the cup of consecrated wine.

The Pope

I have mixed feelings about the pope. Like the government he's a necessary evil. Who is a hero today? Clinton isn't. For more and more people, even for churchmen in the U.S., the pope is not an important issue. This new universal catechism won't overwhelm anyone. People won't read it; preachers won't refer to it. Our allegiance is to money anyhow. I just preached about this. Our motto should be "In money we trust." That's where we hope to find happiness.

Liberal? Radical?

Am I radical? "Radical" is a good word. It means getting to the roots. It depends on the issue. We have to stay open to what's happening. [Censured Swiss theologian] Hans Küng is a hero of mine in theology, and I like Richard McBrien [of the University of Notre Dame] and Avery Dulles [a New York Jesuit]. Among my clerical heroes is Archbishop Weakland of Milwaukee. He's not intimidated. And Bishop Kenneth Untener in Saginaw and Bishop Raymond Lucker in Minnesota. Or in Seattle, Archbishop Raymond Hunthausen or even Archbishop Thomas Murphy there.

They are all much more in line with the Vatican Council than people who make loyalty to the pope a primary virtue. The ambitious ones have to do that. For others it's disgusting. That's not Christ's church. For a primary virtue, I choose compassion as a form of love — that recognizes the woundedness of people.

Authority

On the priests' senate, I sometimes took on the bishop, as once about a diocesan slush fund not honestly reported. It was a custom to skim off 20 percent of any special collection, like for the missions. It never showed up in any reports. I raised Cain about that.

I have written to Rome about priests' celibacy, saying it should be optional. Some priests ignore celibacy. Some who are heroically celibate are an inspiration.

But the present discipline draws the homosexually inclined to the seminary. People trying to be celibate feel out of it. It has led to all that pedophile stuff.

Mandatory celibacy and birth control both take a great toll on church fidelity and membership.

The Fantasy

Yes, churchgoing would plummet. Religion is more difficult today. The nominal faith of the past can't hold up in the face of secular culture and the sense of being demythologized. The more we know about the Bible, for instance, the more complicated is the search for faith.

For Americans in general, not just Catholics, it's one thing to talk about faith, another to have it in your bones. People pick up values through whatever is popular. Television hurts. It debilitates religious acculturation. It makes it harder to have religion in your bones. Even here, only one in four goes to church.

I saw lowered churchgoing in Europe. In France it was 5 to 10 percent when I was a student there. The Dutch church before the council was so strong. Now it's impotent, saddled with conservative bishops imposed by the Vatican. Archconservative people are the only ones who go to church. There's your object lesson.

Chapter 12

Fr. Mahony:
Heading for Hard-Core Christianity

F R. GILBERT MAHONY heads a middle- to upper-middle-class suburban parish of seventeen hundred families in an eastern diocese. A priest for thirty-five years, he has done parish work for all but four or five years in his diocese's religious education office. He's been a pastor for twenty years.

Birth Control

It doesn't come up often. Most handle it themselves. When it comes up, I stress two things that the pope stressed when he reaffirmed the ban: one, that every marriage should be fruitful, whether with ten children or one, and, two, people should be generous in giving themselves to each other. They have to figure out how they can do that best. I leave it at that.

Abortion

I have little contact with women who have had abortions. Now and then someone brings it up, confessing something from her past that still bothers her.

I keep a low profile on the issue. Life is there, and it should be protected. The church ought to be able to educate people not to have abortions. I don't take part in demonstrations. They serve no purpose. I feel concern for the unborn, the defenseless. The church has to be there in some way.

But I am not sure life begins at conception. I have had to examine my position because so many good people are pro-abortion. We Catholics have to examine what we mean by life and when it begins.

Marriage and Divorce

I encounter many invalid marriages. Your article [chapter 1] is interesting. I sympathize with the priest faced with the twice-married Mr. Too-Good to Be True. We all run into that. I encourage annulments and help people get them. If people are open to it, I use internal forum during the process. Our tribunal is good and works hard. But it takes over a year, which is much too long.

If the annulment is denied, I don't perform a ceremony. There's no point to it. The civil marriage is valid even if the sacramental one was not. Anything afterward is to fulfill church legal requirements. It's not that important.

Altar Girls and Women

We've had altar girls for years. I never discussed it with my bishop. The American bishops were foolish to ask the pope about it. It's a stupid question and at the same time a matter of justice to let girls serve mass. I never explained our having girl servers to anybody. I got maybe one letter about it.

I'm very open-minded about women's ordination, but the women on staff keep telling me I'm pretty bad. We try to talk these things over and be sensitive. But women tell me I'm not always as good as I think I am. When you're not, they can do a job on you.

We switched to the Canadian lectionary [book of mass readings] with its inclusive language. A few people commented. Some women didn't like it.

Women are the key ministers. They are the ones who go to church. They take care of everything in the parish. They run the church. But for years they have been discriminated against. It's a matter of recognizing and eliminating that discrimination.

Gays and Lesbians

These issues rarely arise. I consider being gay not natural, if you want to use the term. Same-sex attraction is not normative, and I can't see making it normative. But if it's the only way you can find fulfillment and love in your life, it's okay. I can be sympathetic to an individual, allowing such a person to be part of the church.

The whole question is, are you born gay or made gay? Many are born gay or made gay so early, they have no control over it. Relationships are okay, but they shouldn't be blessed by the church. That's saying it's normal. It isn't. It's an exception.

Liturgy

I found general absolution in this parish and continued the tradition. Then I attended workshops. I heard Fr. Tim O'Connell, a moral theologian at Loyola University, Chicago. According to him, it's more a penitential service with an individual gesture to satisfy the one-on-one requirement. As a service, it works. People find it meaningful in their lives.

People don't come as much to individual confession, just the same few every week. But to a penitential service, three or four hundred come. They look forward to it and like it. It meets the needs of these people. This is what justifies it.

In general, liturgy is powerful because people are familiar with it. You don't have to innovate on your own. My associate pastor, who is a younger priest, is into liturgy and so takes a stricter approach.

The Pope

I disagree with the pope a lot. If he kept out of sex in his teachings, he'd be pretty good. I also disagree with his authoritarian approach. But he's important for the church. Without him we'd be in tough shape. You don't have to believe everything he says. His role is to keep it all together. In the church there is a wide spectrum of beliefs and ways of doing things, from right to left, and he has to say something without people walking off. A lot of what a pope says is done that way, though this one is more conservative than others.

He has to skate a thin line. As Peter Hebblethwaite says in his book on Paul VI, this is the role of a pope, to keep the church together. I try to keep up on where he stands. A lot he puts out is not toe-the-line stuff but for each to apply to one's own situation. He understands that as well as everyone else.

Liberal? Radical?

I have to discern what God wants and say yes to it. That's what's important. All else serves that. Laws are on the books to help us experience God in our life and say yes to him, to help us understand what God is calling us to. It all comes down to me and God, no matter who else is involved.

Authority

Sure, I'd be happy to employ subterfuge for the common good. I work for the bishop, but I also work for the Lord. The bishop is discerning. So am I. If I discern things differently from how he discerns them, I won't do as he asks.

For example, I play down the bishop's insistence that Catholic education is the greatest thing going because I think Catholic schools hurt the church. I am not defying him in this but responding to how I feel and how I must live and work as a priest. The bishop has never questioned this.

The Fantasy

Churchgoing would probably sink to European levels. You can't hold to a hard line. But apart from this, the church must have a core of those who try to live what they believe, who truly believe Jesus makes a difference in their lives. This core serves others for whom belief is not central. A few are committed Christians, but the majority aren't.

That core has to be strong and big enough, so the church can do its work. That's a hard line of another sort — to live that all the way, to be faithful. That's gospel religion, and it's hard to follow.

Chapter 13

Fr. Morgan: Bishop Yes, Pope No

F R. GEORGE MORGAN is a priest of a small western diocese ordained almost twenty-five years. The first pastor he served
with as a newly ordained priest was "a progressive thinker"
who "asked a lot of probing questions." From this and a variety
of workshops, he was "very definitely schooled in Vatican II,"
as were many priests of his generation.

There was "a lot of openness" among them, but he says that
has changed, and many of the young priests and religious are
more conservative. To a younger nun who "wants to freeze
the process," he said recently, "I question your fidelity to the
church. I don't think I'm not traditional."

He heads a parish of about one thousand families in a rural
town of fifteen thousand or so; with its environs, forty thousand to fifty thousand. The parish is "basically America" —
wealthy, middle-class, and poor. Many are Mexican-Americans.
Its membership "cuts across all lines."

Birth Control

When people ask, I try to lead them to a decision in conscience.
The focus on conscience is important. I speak in terms of com-
peting values. It's "tension morality" as I learned years ago in
an article I read in the seminary, by a Sulpician priest. You have
to pick one value and not the other. You're in a state of tension.

For people with a large family, it's a question of the love of
husband and wife and the problem sexual abstinence causes in
their relationship. It's also a question of following the church's

94

teaching about the sexual act being open to life. If you choose one, you downplay the other. So you try to build each up in some way. If you don't choose the church's teaching, you try to build up your loyalty to the church in other ways. If you choose it, you build up your marital relationship in other ways. You make up for the choice in either case.

I say sex should be open to life and love. The disagreement is whether each and every act must be open to that. Some say being open in general is enough. I say you must avoid the contraceptive mentality and be open to God.

I feel the church is wrong about this each-and-every-act business. I also think most people have decided. The more the pope pushes the point, the less credible he is. It hurts his authority.

Moreover, this teaching is not on solid theological ground. It's severely questioned, in fact. The encyclical *Humanae Vitae* [by Paul VI in 1968, reaffirming the prohibition] says good stuff about human life. But it uses the same old, discredited arguments. One priest I know said he never was asked to follow a position based solely on the authority of the church.

My Mexican parishioners, simple people, practice birth control after seven or eight kids, taking the pill and worrying about going to hell. I speak pretty good Spanish, and I discuss it with them. But I can't get anywhere. They are not used to making their own decisions of conscience. They want me to say yes or no. My approach may be too sophisticated for them.

Abortion

I'm very much with the church on abortion. But a priest friend questions the whole thing, asking, "Is an acorn an oak?"

"If it isn't," I say, "it's ordained to become one."

Most in our parish oppose abortion but are pro-choice, using the typically American argument that people have the right to make their own decision. They say the woman has the right to make her choice, though they disapprove of the choice for abortion. Some even say that if their daughter were in a certain situation, they would be hard-pressed not to go along with her.

Not many are pro-choice in the liberal style, disagreeing with the church on the morality issue. At the same time, not many are radically against abortion. I don't preach about it, except on Respect Life Sunday. Then I mention it as one of many pro-life issues, according to Cardinal Joseph Bernardin's consistent ethic of life approach, which also opposes capital punishment and euthanasia.

I taught a class on what I called "modern moral issues." I discussed the state of the question with thirty or forty people, starting with the role of conscience and how to form your conscience. My goal was for them at least to know the church's position and the reasons for it — on abortion, birth control, euthanasia, and capital punishment.

I found myself way over my head because I'm not a theologian. Areas are so complex, like cutting off life supports and the like. I said, "Look at the teaching." We came to no conclusions, but people enjoyed it. It was an open forum, the only one of its kind for them. And over my head or not, it was the right place for me to be as a pastor.

I don't really have an abortion ministry, except to encourage people to become informed and to support ministries that give options to abortion.

Marriage and Divorce

I run into bad marriages regularly, especially among candidates for baptism. It's a key part of my ministry, the hardest issue we deal with apart from death and suffering. I always start with annulment, describing and explaining the process. They should be introduced to the church as it is, not as how I would like it to be.

But for some the process would unearth the distant past. They are in a stable marriage and going through the experience of faith and the desire to live a good life. But they were married before, and there's no way the church can annul it. To a couple married fifteen or twenty years, am I to say it's not a marriage?

Plus there's the pain of the process. I ask, How can God be calling and not calling someone at the same time to a deeper life in the church? But they are bound by a prior vow and so forth. At that point I explain that if we can't go through the annulment process, we can talk of a good-conscience case. I say it's not official recognition of their marriage, but we are dealing directly with God.

"If you feel you're clear with God," I say, "God won't condemn you. Neither will I condemn you. If you want to receive the Eucharist, do so."

Is there scandal? Most say it's about time so-and-so started to receive communion. Most don't cause problems by receiving. But it's a tough one. It took me a long time to see it. I came around by the example of a priest I respected, plus experience.

I decided the people I knew couldn't be living in sin. I couldn't see why they were denied the sacraments. The deprivation caused them great suffering. I could not authoritatively say the prior marriage was invalid, but I could say this is a marriage. Why deny them the Eucharist?

What are we preserving here? Not the first marriage, which is over. Are we saving Jesus from them? But they seem in such need of the consolations of the Eucharist. That's how I came to this position. Rarely it happens that I can't do it.

Altar Girls and Women

We have no altar girls. The bishop wrote a four-page letter telling us not to have them, saying we were to dismiss the ones we had. I didn't dismiss any, but I got no more. It was a dumb thing for him to do. It's ridiculous. Women distribute the Eucharist and are lectors at mass. They do about 95 percent of the ministry. Why can't they do this?

The only reason I don't have altar girls is it's not one of the issues I will go to the wall for, bucking the bishop.

Will girl servers want to be priests? It doesn't work that way with boys. I wish it did.

Not that there's much call for girl servers. I am thinking of talking to the new bishop about it, asking him how he would handle it. I don't think he'll have a problem.

Another prohibition is that we're not supposed to have outdoor weddings. I tell the brides it's an issue bishops and brides care too much about.

I think the arguments against ordaining women don't hold water. Women perform most of the ministry as it is. Some who want to be priests can also be power-hungry, but it's not a hot topic here. We have some very thoughtful women in our parish.

They care about this but are not vehement or cynical. There are no radical feminist approaches here.

Gays and Lesbians

The problem doesn't come up much. I got a letter from a gay man leaving our parish. "Grateful for the hope you have given me," he wrote. He and I had talked about it. He's living a good Catholic life. He sang in our choir. I didn't turn him away. He had been transferred here from a big city, where he had found a parish and had been worried about what he would find here. But he was very pleased with what he found here.

The town has just a few gay people who are open. They are accepted. One of them hears the latest from the pope and gets angry and won't come around. Politics is local, but what the church says universally affects people.

I don't have a gay ministry as such. I have never thought about it. This man asked if I'd say mass an hour's drive away on a Saturday for a "special group," but he didn't ask me to form a gay and lesbian group as such. Maybe they have decided they are not welcome. But I never turn anybody away. I would never do that. I'm sure they have made decisions about where they stand.

Liturgy

I don't do much that's unauthorized. I don't feel the need for it. What's allowed has been effective. My goal is to do it as it's meant to be done. I did a lot of that creative stuff as a young priest. I did rock masses, had banners in the aisles, used different readings, changed the order around. I don't know how effective it was.

I prefer a penitential service which includes individual confessions, a priest in the sanctuary and a few others in confessionals. People don't give a laundry list but mention one area they want to express sadness about. Absolution is individual and instant. There's no time for questioning. Counseling is for another time. It's a tradeoff. The whole thing is very powerful.

I have not found a need for the unauthorized. Little things work, like how to focus the opening hymn, what involves people and is nourishing — simple things. Do what's there and do it well is my rule. Being creative doesn't mean going outside the rules, but taking full advantage of what's there.

The Pope

He's a tough one. He has done some wonderful things. He was one of the prime movers in the demise of communism in Eastern Europe. It seems that's why he was chosen by the Holy Spirit. I don't know his effect on the church around the world. I'm pretty provincial, so I can't comment on that, except about communism. He certainly has made the papacy a strong player on the world stage.

But within the church, I have not found him helpful. He stands for a return to a style of church I thought we had put away. The Vatican Council produced an awakening. It was the beginning of a church with a different model, according to which people would listen to each other. This pope has tried to turn us back to the authoritarian church of old. That's my biggest problem with him.

He doesn't listen in some areas. The teacher who listens is far more effective. He can say anything he wants to say: "Here's our position." But he never asks.

And he has created a climate in which right-wing Catholic groups play a bigger role than they should. He's divisive. It's profoundly disappointing, very sad.

He's a wonderful, charismatic man, but he's not helping my ministry. We're at cross purposes. He and the Vatican he has created do not come across as credible. His ministry is not helpful within the church, at least in this country. A lot of priests feel the same way. People my age feel disheartened, disillusioned.

People read the paper, hear a squib, and say, "Same old stuff. Why should I bother?"

He is making bishops who want to rise higher or whose only concern is that everyone observe orthodox teaching. Some new ones in my area are very pastoral, however, if theologically conservative. Being pastoral is what's important.

Others make big issues over altar girls and birth control. They further alienate people on the fringes who have dismissed the church for one reason or another, giving them more reason to dismiss it.

I just disregard what he says, as in sexual areas. This is where the church lacks a credible voice. The church has a lot to offer, but there has to be some sense that he has paid attention to what is happening: "I know the suffering, but here's what we're faced with." That sort of thing. The church must appear to understand daily problems.

He seems to have little to say to people, when in fact the church has a lot to say. We should be hearing solid sexual morality that leads people away from license and promiscuity.

My problems are in helping people to live their life every day, just the things we are talking about — sex in and out of marriage, people living together. These are the issues we face. I don't appreciate his tightening up, his authoritarian, top-down style.

I don't know if I'm loyal to the pope, or how loyal he is to us. Some right-wing people say we are not loyal to the church. I say, how do they think the church got to this point where it became the church they are loyal to? What they take for granted was brought to this point by a process of development of doctrine and of deeper understanding.

Liberal? Radical?

The liberal-conservative difference might not be a thing of the past. I think of the TV nun Mother Angelica lashing out, saying liberal Catholics should leave the church. She's a menace, with her stridency and right-wing fundamentalism. It's a piece of religion I don't like. It's more rampant in our church, partly because this pope has created a climate for it.

Authority

I don't defy the bishop. Our current bishop is very good. I had one earlier I didn't get along with, but that was because of his personal style. That's when it's difficult. I don't see myself as defying authority. There's no need to, at least in our diocese.

It's not my ideal to be known as an obedient person, but

sometimes it's convenient to have a diocesan policy to refer to, to be able to tell people this is not just my own thinking.

It's been very enjoyable to work here under our last two bishops. There's not a lot of authoritarianism in our diocese and no need for subterfuge.

It's a smaller diocese and so maybe more relaxed for that reason. The bishop says, "If there's a problem, tell me." That helps. If you feel you're heard, it makes a difference. He has a collaborative style. He's theologically conservative, but he works with us. I wish the papacy had the same style.

The Fantasy

Eventually I will retire and hand this over. If we did not budge, we would have far fewer people. I don't know where we are going now, to be honest. In a couple of generations, there could be very few people at church.

As a parish priest, I want the church to be a support for people as they live their lives. I resist the hard line because it does not nourish people.

The whole reason the Vatican Council was called was that we wondered if we were losing touch with our people. To go back is to create a bubble, all in its place, happy with our doctrine, but not saying a thing to people trying to live their lives every day. I don't see conservative parishes growing.

Read the journal *Chicago Studies* on parishes. The pastor of the nondenominational Willow Creek Church, in Barrington, Illinois, says half his congregation are Catholics. That's what's going to happen. If needs are not fulfilled in the Catholic Church, people will go somewhere else.

Leave my name out of it. I am not interested in discussing these things with a lot of people. My mentor, an older priest who thinks this way, is not even interested in being interviewed. He's fought all these battles. No more.

Chapter 14

Fr. Pfleger: Rebel with Cause

F R. MICHAEL PFLEGER heads St. Sabina's, a nine-hundred-family African-American parish on Chicago's South Side. The parish supports itself with Sunday collections ranging from $8,000 to $11,000. The school has 505 students, 75 more than a year ago. There's a new black-top parking lot, and the gym was renovated a year ago at a cost of $100,000.

He has been pastor since 1981, when he was only six years out of seminary. Such early elevation would have been unthinkable a few decades earlier, and least of all at St. Sabina's, a keystone parish of the once-white South Side, not far from the "Irish, Catholic, and Democratic" Chicago neighborhood where he grew up. He has never been anywhere else in his eighteen years as a priest.

Martin Luther King's daughter, Berniece King, preached there as a Protestant seminary student. The notorious Louis Farrakhan, the Muslim leader who once called Judaism a "gutter religion," has preached there twice, in 1988 and in the summer of 1993, in each case during mass at homily time.

"People can have a lot of problems with Minister Farrakhan, but he stands on what he believes and believes by the word," said Fr. Pfleger, presumably referring to the word as found in the Koran. "People flock to him because they respect his integrity."

At St. Sabina's "we take the Scriptural standpoint," he said, sitting at a plain wooden conference table that he pounded periodically for emphasis. He talked about the Word of God like an evangelical preacher. As rule-benders go, he's strict.

102

Birth Control

I teach that if people walk with the Lord, whatever their circumstance, God won't put on them what they can't handle. I tell them that once a couple has come to a certain faith point, they don't need birth control. If they have not reached this point, they should decide for themselves what to do. They should pray to God, saying, "We're not ready. Make us ready."

In counseling couples, I say they are to decide for themselves as a couple. I never talk about it to husband or wife separately.

Abortion

I recognize no right to take life, whether in the womb or by capital punishment or by war or any other means. So I am dead against abortion, with the possible exception of a rape case. To girls considering abortion, I say, "You have made one mistake, don't make two." But I can't say I would say that to the rape victim.

I'm not in the right-to-life movement because its emphasis is on legal questions. I'm for teaching about the body as a temple and about the dignity of human life, womb to tomb. Right-to-life people are riled up about that womb but not about racism or economic injustice. They deal with bringing a baby into the world but not with what happens if the baby is black or brown.

Our mistake has been we have not talked about the dignity and value of human life across the board. Racism is as evil as abortion, but we don't say so. We are not consistent.

Marriage and Divorce

I find a lot of bad marriages, but in the last three years, there's been a turnaround here. To people shacking up together, I have been saying you can't do that and come to this church. We are going back to saying, "Here are the standards. Not necessarily Catholic standards, but according to God's word. You may fall short, but this is what you are to be reaching for. So you should not feel comfortable shacking up and coming here on Sunday."

The sexually active couple who want me to marry them must stop. If they are living together, one of them must move out.

Then they must be active in our church for at least six months while living apart.

Married couples help to prepare couples for marriage and provide a strong support ministry to couples. They do this much better than I can.

Marriage is under attack today, from Satan or evil or whatever you want to call it, and we must be prepared. People should be scripturally prepared to be godly husbands and wives, to live together as a manifestation of the oneness of the Trinity.

Standard marriage preparation programs haven't prepared people scripturally. It takes a lot of examining of the Word to prepare a wife and husband for their Christian walk together.

I turned down probably twenty couples last year because they weren't ready. Some were at peace with that. Others went to another Catholic church, where they were married, sometimes as soon as two weeks later.

We must prepare people. It's easy for a priest to do his two little set classes. But if I'm going to bring these two before the church and before God, I'm accountable. I am not going to lie on those papers and say they are ready if I think they're not.

Altar Girls and Women

We have altar girls, and women preach here. Women should be ordained. Mary was the first to preach the good news, bringing word of the resurrection. But we're caught in tradition and "religionism." There's nothing wrong with tradition, except when it gets in the way of the word. We should not determine who God calls to ordination. It is ours to prepare and help discern the call, not to make it.

Gays and Lesbians

The gay and lesbian question is not dealt with openly in the black community. When someone comes for counseling, as a parent concerned about his or her child, I refer the person to someone gifted in that area. That's my style. When I have not had training in an area, I send people to someone who has had training. I am not all things to all. Father is supposed to know everything. That's garbage. We screwed more people up that way.

Liturgy

We keep the basic structure, liturgy of the word and of the Eucharist. But you have to bring people to a desire for the Eucharist. You have to set a fire in them. So we have a very strong word service, in contrast to a lot of Catholic churches, where the word is weakened and people rely entirely on the Eucharist. Ninety percent of our people bring Bibles and notebooks.

In addition, we have two Bible study sessions a week, drawing 50 to 150 people, and a third is to start soon.

I object to how the church picks and chooses from the Bible, cafeteria-style. You can't pick and choose and quote isolated passages, as some do. You have to know the whole Bible, give correct teaching, use good exegesis, something not often done in preaching.

I teach the Bible as the word of God, not as a nice little book of reference. The word comes first. The liturgy is how we ritualize it. I teach the word first and then how the Catholic Church seeks to support the word.

Some of our masses reflect African-American culture, but others you could do anywhere. I'm not caught up in the demands of ritual. It's not as important that people say "Glory to God in the highest" as that they actually give glory to God at that point.

We do it singing, with people throughout the church raising hands, praising and worshiping God aloud. It's drawing the Spirit into place, calling on the anointing of God and God's presence, entering into the presence of God.

You can't just have the opening song and bam! you're in the presence of God. People are coming from all different things in their lives. They have to arrive at a unity, bring themselves into God's presence. Some Sundays our praise and worship goes for an hour and a half, before we even get to the first reading.

The 11:15 Sunday morning service goes normally to 2:30, sometimes to 3:30. But people are less concerned about time than about quality. In fact, the longest service is the best attended. What people look for is to learn something and realize they are changed by what they experienced.

Thirty percent of our members are Catholics who returned to the church after seven or more years. They left fed up or not well fed in a spiritual sense, some for other denominations. They returned in part because of the parish's high profile. Another 15 to 20 percent were raised Protestant, which is unusual for a Catholic parish.

The Pope

I feel no disloyalty toward the pope. I respect him and consider him very holy. I have been impressed with his U.S. appearances, as in Denver. But I consider absolutely intolerable his ban on discussion of women's ordination. When you won't discuss something, something is wrong. It's a bizarre approach.

My bigger concern is with the hierarchy in general, who are more concerned about church law than about God's law. The church is no longer a voice in the wilderness but a corporation. We are called to renew the face of the earth, but we can't renew it if we look just like it.

We constantly look at the financial thing, but God is not a bankrupt God. When we get back to doing God's work and holding to God's standards, then will we flourish.

We don't command respect any more. In most Catholic churches, you can be a racist and receive communion with no problem. You can be a thief at your job, cheat on your wife, hate your next-door neighbor, and feel no contradiction in all that. Something is wrong.

Our leadership is disastrous. How can you call your people to a relationship with the Lord when there's no such relationship in your own life? It's spiritual bankruptcy. We're in trouble.

Liberal? Radical?

I'm not radical. The gospel is radical. If you seek to live by the gospel, you will have troubles. I will fight and die for what I believe in. I've been jailed thirty-some times for protests, like against liquor and cigarette advertising on billboards in black neighborhoods. People hate me. I have a police bodyguard because of all the threats I have received.

John the Baptist was killed for what he said. Jesus said some radical things. Paul? Everywhere he went, there was turmoil and riots. Christianity is an invading force.

Being liberal means you don't get hung up on traditional things, like couples not living together. God doesn't come in to take sides on liberal and radical. He comes in to take over.

Authority

I recognize the cardinal is my boss, though at times I do things without asking, knowing that if I did ask, he would say no. But I try to respect authority.

I say some critical things, that the archdiocese and its school system are racist. Some priests tell me, "If you're so critical, why not leave?" I say, "Why don't *you* leave?"

I have always told the cardinal, "If you tell me to leave this parish, I will leave." But I must be obedient to the work. I believe we are more Catholic here than most Catholic churches, more faithful to our Catholic origins.

I may not press people to understand the sacrament of confession as some want me to. But our people know what forgiveness is. They know they cannot receive any blessing from God as long as there's unforgiveness in them. They know that repentance is changing your heart and ways.

The Fantasy

I'm not a hard-liner on ritual, but I am on the word. What I tell people is based on the gospel rather than on the latest from Rome, which has to support the word.

Chapter 15

Fr. Nolan:
Permission No, Forgiveness Yes

FR. DONALD NOLAN does family life work in an eastern diocese. He was ordained almost forty years ago and has worked in parishes for most of those years. He's an old hand, with a ready laugh.

Birth Control

I do a lot of marriage preparation work and agree with most of the social science research that people are deciding birth control for themselves. It's not put to priests as it once was. The whole understanding of sexuality is different today. But church law does not reflect this.

In my work we put marriage preparation in a context of the natural family planning philosophy. We get away from the unfeeling "gotcha" God who makes a lot of laws and throws you into hell as quickly as possible.

People don't observe the law. Sometimes they can't. That doesn't mean they are bad people. But they don't explicitly reject the law either. The assumption is, it's easier to get forgiveness than to get permission.

Abortion

Our pro-life perspective is well known, so people don't ask us what our stance is, though they may ask us to explain it. We spend a lot of time fighting rigid pro-life people condemning us for being pro-abortion. They say we refer people to Planned Parenthood. We don't.

I call myself a reasonable anti-abortionist. I have no problem discussing and cooperating with others not on my side. I don't treat them as murderers. On a whole array of issues, we cooperate with family agencies across the state that I'm sure are pro-choice. I don't think that's bending any rules at all.

Marriage and Divorce

In the inner city, where I did parish work, survival was the issue and many didn't even have state blessings on their marriages. When people began to "practice" their religion, as we say, we could talk. I would discover that among Latinos there had been serial marriages, but with neither license nor church service. So there were no bonds to break. I never granted a declaration of nullity on my own. But it's not uncommon among priests I know in suburban parishes.

Altar Girls and Women

Altar girls and the women question don't belong in the same sentence. Altar girls is wine-and-water stuff. It's over anyway. It's not an issue any more. Where I live and do weekend work — mass, preaching, confessions — there's no distinction between wine-and-water work and the rest that women do. But the two don't go together.

I favor women's ordination, but I can't discuss it with my bishop, who considers it a litmus test of correct doctrine and practice.

Gays and Lesbians

If I stay away from the question of living together and the public marriage ceremony, I have no problem. My problem is with permanent sexual partners. I haven't worked that out for myself. At a recent Catholic funeral of an AIDS victim, the man's partner was in the front pew. As pastor I'd permit this. I don't think we should judge things.

I don't disagree with church law, frankly. In my AIDS ministry, I try to work with a person as long and hard as I can, to keep him alive and in the church. I have been much involved in recent years. The ones I've met I have found to be pretty special people. And talented. My gracious, how talented. I'm in admiration of many of them.

Liturgy

Innovating has a wide range. In the seminary we had our hands pounded flat on the altar as required, and the number of signs of the cross we made was monitored. But liturgy is an attitude and a sense of involving everybody in the prayer. So some unauthorized things seem appropriate.

There's a difference between the "macro church," on Sundays, and the "micro church," as in groups gathered for Engaged Encounter, a marriage-preparation program. For micro there are no rules or regulations. And there's enabling legislation for it. Not for crazy things but for theatrical things in good taste. So you preach in center aisle for better contact and give different kinds of homilies. It has its own style of music. There's freedom now I didn't have at the start of my ministry.

But people still don't want to be surprised. So, routine and respect for tradition are very important. You learn some things as you go along. People tell you what they like and don't like. The homily is the key. It must be done well.

The Pope

I have problems with stereotypes of the pope. He's trying to do his best. To his social encyclicals I say, "Right on." But in other matters, he's trying to control things. Some of it is a little scary to me. There's some anti-Polish ethnicity in me that says, "What does he know?" The Vatican bureaucracy is a problem.

He's pastoral, as he was with the youth this summer, and he has a human side that's pretty special. But he's also trying to control my life as I lead it in the U.S. in this diocese. That's pretty unreal.

Liberal? Radical?

Law without spirit is not Christianity, as far as I'm concerned. I'm more the humanist today than when I was ordained. That makes me somewhat of a radical. I'm considered a radical around here. I don't try to hide behind churchy things. I'm not interested in becoming a monsignor. I really don't care. I seem to be fairly well accepted by all sides. Rather than a liberal vs. radical spectrum, I prefer rigid vs. free-flowing or human. I try not to be too rigid.

Authority

I don't ask for permissions much any more, even less so given our new bishop. Control is important to him. The best offense is "Come and catch me." Or as a friend told me, "Donald, this is not the time to be seen." If the bishop wants to know what I'm doing, all he has to do is call. But the only call will be when he hears about a radical action of mine or if I'm in trouble with politics or someone's wife.

Retaliation? Yeah, I fear it. I don't want to be called in either for wearing a necktie. So I don't wear a necktie. It's not important enough. Life is bigger.

The Fantasy

I think we'd drive almost everybody away with a hard line. It's "Do as I say, not as I do." We have to read the gospel a little more.

As for the church of the future, there's a small-community movement across the country. Large suburban, filling-station kinds of church are out of it. Hospitality and intimacy are important in all the surveys, Andrew Greeley's among them. We have to find ways to attract people and get personal with them. Then we can preach the gospel.

The material on evangelization is all counter to the moral and doctrinal purity stuff. Preaching pure doctrine gets to be pharisaical. You're not going to lasso people and tie 'em up and bring 'em into church. That's medieval. There's no baptizing Shylock at the end, as in *The Merchant of Venice*.

Chapter 16

Fr. McNamee: The Corporal Works

FR. JOHN P. MCNAMEE is pastor of mostly black St. Malachy's parish in inner-city Philadelphia. In his book *Diary of a City Priest,* a daily journal for 1991 recently published by Sheed and Ward, he describes what he calls "The Margins of the Church."

"My presence in these neighborhoods is in part self-interest," he writes. "I am here because this is as much Church as I can handle." He means the "tribal church" of clerical appointments and politics and fund-raising, as opposed to "gospel church."

In a telephone conversation, he expanded on the church-margin issue.

I've been in inner-city work for twenty-five years. One of its dimensions has been that questions requiring this kind of discernment, bending the rules, do not come up. People don't ask sexual questions. Life is more basic here. I try to get folks jobs, which is more and more difficult. I get people detoxed, so they can get rehabilitated. It's a world of women and children, with no marriages and no Catholics.

That's all the more reason for the church to be here, in the spirit of Scriptures. My ministry is providing emergency food and shelter.

But one could also say a reason for my being here is that it removes me from the intramural world where these questions are debated and even anguish people's lives. Maybe early on, one decides to go into these neighborhoods that have little to do with traditional Catholicism, where one is free of that kind of question.

112

That's not to belittle that kind of question. Maybe I'm more comfortable here because of the respect I have for our tradition. In another work, I would be expected to be free-wheeling, but very little bending is required here.

A while back, I attended the fancy wedding of old friends. A woman guest whom I did not know, alerted by my clerical garb, her tongue loosened a bit by drinks, began telling me about how much she had suffered in her life from the sexual ethics she learned in her convent school days. She did it publicly. It was a confrontation with me as a persona of the church.

When she finished, I didn't know what to say, except that what's behind Catholic sex ethics is that sex doesn't work outside of marriage. I said that everything in my experience in these neighborhoods has made me fairly comfortable with that understanding, including the disarray that comes from the absence of family life. Bringing children into the world outside of the family seems hardly to work. I had not much more to say on the subject.

The social justice agenda surfaces very clearly here. A lot of the problems sending people to my rectory door in droves will hardly be resolved without serious attention to social issues and social justice.

Even now, we have nuclear subs, I read with dismay in a recent *Commonweal*. The arms race works against the poor and deprives them of bread and housing and work, decent schools, and many other things.

You can quote me. I give the okay with bated breath. The Catholic Worker house here began recently to take on the archdiocese about inner-city closings. I had helped bring the Worker people back here after an absence and had been in on planning with them for two years.

Interviewed by a young reporter, I told about Dorothy Day and showed him something she had written in which she made a nuanced reference in biblical terms to the church as a harlot. Next day, the headline read, "Church is a harlot, says inner-city priest."

Chapter 17

Fr. Sanders and Fr. Lewis:
Feisty and Funny

FR. BEN SANDERS AND FR. WALT LEWIS were ordained in the 1960s. Both head parishes now, one suburban, the other a city parish, both in Midwestern middle-class neighborhoods.

Birth Control

"Nobody asks about it. It's the pope's question," said Fr. Ben.

"Does he think God wants it?" asked Fr. Walt.

And what about natural family planning, the approved periodic-abstinence method based on presumably more accurate information than the old thermometer method?

"I am asked why I don't mention it," said Walt. "But it seems naive. You want to preserve a certain credibility. Let a sort of flat-earth theory onto the podium, and you lose some credibility."

"You feel foolish," said Ben. "Items come for use in the bulletin, and I put them in there. It's a low-key way to offer exposure to a part of today's church, a part I think is nonsense. But if 3 percent of the people are passionately in favor of something, they have a right to be acknowledged."

Should there be more from the pulpit about sex in marriage, encouraging it as a good thing?

"The homily is to connect Scripture with life, rather than to cover topics," said Ben.

"And sex doesn't come up in the Gospels," said Walt.

"Jesus never talked about birth control," said Ben. "Of course he may have been severely edited by his followers."

Abortion

Ben has dealt with a few women who have had abortions and were feeling remorse years later. But it doesn't come up, "except from pro-life people who are past the age of having children and want to make sure everybody else has them. It's academic in my ministry.

"What do I think about it? The only true Christian position is pro-life. Which is more than abortion, and I think abortion is a tragedy. But the answer is not to pass all kinds of laws. It's a matter of perceiving the value of life itself. As seminarians we were taught abortion is wrong because the child was there at conception. We know now that's not true. And there's a lot more we don't know."

"Abortion is a problem and an issue," said Walt. "Through Project Rachel, people are sent to us who have had abortions. This addresses the problem.

"As an issue, it's more a project or activity. You give parish activists rope and let them run with it, or you integrate them into your peace and justice committee, as part of the pro-life spectrum.

"But pro-lifers have nothing in common with the peace and justice people at our place. We planned a dialog on capital punishment. Fine, I told the planners, but nobody will come. And nobody came.

"We had one on abortion, and forty-five or so came. We were all on our guard. I used 'civil' and 'civility' a lot. In the end there was a lot of disagreement, but people were still civil to each other. It was an exercise in civility. Usually, on abortion, nobody is willing to let others say anything.

"Not that any minds were changed. One guy said he went from pro-life to pro-choice, but that was twelve years ago. Everybody thought that was amazing, that someone had changed his mind."

Marriage and Divorce

"We had a parish school alumni reunion," said Walt. "There was a lot of drinking, apparently a revisiting of goofy childhood patterns. I got over there late. A lot were mellow.

"One man came at me. 'I got this friend,' he said. 'Like a sister to me. Never married, marrying this guy who was married twice before. We're forty-five now. It would be a dirty shame if she got married anywhere else but here. We know that's decided at the local level now. I just wanted to know, how is your local level here?'

" 'Never married, like a sister to me,' he said. 'You don't want her to get married at a marriage chapel down the block, do you?' he said. I said, 'Have her call me.'

"Once my standards were pretty clear. I would have said I can't do it. I don't know what my standards are now. If the man doesn't want an annulment, he can't be married. That would have been my position. But I think the guy at the reunion is right. It would be wrong for her to get married down the block. Whatever hold the church has on her now, even if nostalgic, would be terrible to abuse, to say, 'You're out,' automatically.

"So if she calls, I will ask them to come in. I will try to have an intelligent conversation with them. And not about the legalities. And this sounds really foolish, but I wouldn't want the legalities to be the determining factor. The guy is right. It's determined on the local level, or it should be. How you do that, I don't know."

Ben spoke. "I'm at a point of confusion now. People come looking for a wider dimension to the ending of their marriage than what the two of them provide. They see it as a sacrament in which the community is involved. In which the church is involved. For them it's important that somehow the church recognize and accept the fact that their earlier marriage is over.

"These are not institutionally dependent people. Some are very thoughtful and mature. Some want to remarry, some don't. One partner seeks the annulment even when no other potential partner is in sight yet. 'My marriage was between him and me and God and the church,' one might say. 'If it breaks up, I have to bring God into it.' These are mature folks. They don't come in because they 'gotta come.' They want this."

They signed on with the church, now they feel they should sign off with it?

"Yes, it might be at the local level, however that's done. They say they want the church involved. The term 'Catholic divorce' is flippant. There's a church-and-God dimension to marriage."

They want the church to validate their marriage's dissolution? To say there never was a marriage?

"Never a relationship, people say. Two different things. People seeking annulment explain that the partner was incapable of living the intimate life. They didn't see it before. Now they see it. Everybody knows a marriage requires the capacity for intimacy. It's a relief for people to realize the other was not capable. 'I didn't see that,' they say, 'and I shouldn't beat myself over the head for this.'"

Can you be too legalistic about it?

"'In the eyes of the church' says it," said Walt. "A woman told me she had just found out her husband had been married when she married him. She wanted me to cross it out of the book. She said nothing about going downtown. I crossed it out and told her, 'It's out.' That was enough for her. Black lady, real intelligent. She said nothing about what this does to her children, her relationship, and the rest. In the eyes of the church, her marriage was no longer recognized. In the eyes of the local church, that is, where it's in the book."

The civil process has its role, mainly in handling property?

"The church got involved in legal fictions," said Walt.

"From when it was the only legal entity, centuries ago," said Ben. "Not until the twelfth century was a priest witness required for sacramental validity. 'In the eyes of the church' says it. Am I a member in good standing? Does this organization like me? Am I okay?"

The church is a great validating instrument then? The church dignified the relationship. Wouldn't it be nice if the church were to recognize it's not there any more, de-dignify it?

"This is done by the marriage tribunal, where good men sometimes find themselves defeated," said Walt. "Tribunal lawyers try to make the institution work for people and find it's useless. It gets to them. They get officious or start losing heart. I saw a guy lose heart that way. He died bitter and crabbed."

"This is not peculiar to the church," said Ben. "The higher

you go in a structure, the less freedom you have. As you move up, the consequences of departing from policy are greater."

Altar Girls and Women

Walt spoke of "a scale of daring," a measurement of how "downtown," the chancery, "rates things scandal-wise." At the high end of the scale would be witnessing the same-sex marriage of another pastor. This would put scandal "off the charts." Having altar girls, on the other hand, requires "almost no daring, unless you're so literal-minded, you're a moron."

He and Ben could think of only one pastor who had banned altar girls — "a committed Mariologist out about twenty years."

Ben had heard of a visiting priest, on hand to say a funeral mass for a relative, who on seeing altar girls told the pastor, "Send the girls home. You're not supposed to have them, and I don't need them."

"These girls are members of my parish, and you're not," said the pastor. "I'll take the funeral, and you can leave."

"People feel very territorial," commented Ben.

Is parish identity the issue?

"It's a women's issue," said Ben. "Most Catholics are women. Most who go to mass and join organizations are women. And women are leaving left and right. Can you imagine a church with all men? Jesus, Mary, and Joseph. It would be a small group that didn't do much."

"Inclusive language is a problem," said Walt. "Its proponents bug you sometimes. Frankly, it becomes a bothersome thing. How it's done makes a big difference."

"I was once referred to as the only man in a group," said Ben. "A woman said, 'We're all men. We've been called men all our life!'

"A lot of priests and deacons are good at using inclusive language on the fly. But as pastor I want to draw others into the practice, make it staff policy, get it to the liturgy committee, so at least they know why we do it."

"Women's advocacy is intense in the church, because of a certain maleness of structure," said Walt. "So working with women on a parish staff, a man runs into this, facing legitimate gripes. The world is male-dominated, and they let you know it."

"The number of pastoral associates [almost all women] has dropped sharply in the diocese," said Ben. "One reason is economics, but it's not the only reason. A number of women find it very difficult to work with priests in the parish. It may be their fault, but my hunch is it isn't. It's probably an unconscious sexist approach they run into.

"Church imagery is male-dominated. It's very narrow. It gets hard to breathe, it's so relentless. For imagery reasons alone, a lot of women don't go to mass as often as they used to. Just count the male images in mass prayers, including the Eucharistic prayer. The average person would be surprised."

Gays and Lesbians

In an earlier parish where Ben served, "it became difficult to tell who was gay and who wasn't. I found it healthy," he said. "A lot of the leaders were known as gays and lesbians. But it wasn't an issue. People were proud of that. You could make it an issue if you tried to exclude them. But most gays and lesbians are not public about it, so no one knows."

"I'm a believer in the new numbers" showing only 2 percent or 3 percent of the population as homosexual, said Walt — "a lot fewer than we have been led to believe. In the ordinary parish, only 2 percent or 3 percent are gay, so it's not a big problem. In the priesthood, on the other hand, it's way higher. There are going to be two priesthoods, and very soon, because of the split between straights and gays.

"We pretend we don't notice, but there are big differences between the two groups. Both sides understand this, but no one wants to think it. It's going to be a gigantic issue in the church."

What shape will it take? Turf protection, mutual suspicion?

"Already there's suspicion. Turf issues haven't surfaced, because most of it is closeted. You can't have turf if you're closeted. There will be an exposé or outing. It will be explosive. Downtown won't, doesn't know how to deal with it. It's going to blow up in their face. People have asked them to deal with it, and they haven't."

Outing and coming out would involve pastor-parishioner problems too?

"Yes."

Have you any percentages?

"No. I am amazed that people can come up with, say, 40 percent. But my knowledge is limited, partly because gay priests stay away from non-gay priests. I don't even know who they are."

Ben conceded the numbers could be high, as reported from various sources. "The priesthood makes it acceptable for two men to travel together. It offers a cover, institutionalizes the male relationship.

"But it's really a matter of the Catholic obsession with sex. We have created the problem, and the people who will pay for it are gay. We have brought this on ourselves."

"I don't know about that," said Walt. "A certain softness and effeminacy has happened in the church. I don't know how it's connected to homosexuality. Our diocese has the best leadership we could hope for. But even the bishop projects a softness."

"I like him a lot, but it's people like him who can get ahead in the system," said Ben.

"That's a problem, when you have this softness," said Walt. "It's probably in some way connected to homosexuality as a given in the church. Unless the whole thing is faced, you allow softness to be the real mode the church is known for.

"Once the pastor in this diocese was known as cigar-chomping and whiskey-drinking. How did that change? I think that it is connected somehow to not facing certain things, like homosexuality."

How would it have been faced?

"Congress faced it. Representative Barney Frank [Dem., Mass.] stood up, admitted it, people approved. In the '40s and '50s here, the cover-up was for drinking. It's not that any more. It's this other stuff."

"It's a matter of valuing the person as a person," said Ben. "We didn't do that in the '40s and '50s. A priest could be crude and rude. One told a group of women, 'If you have a miscarriage, bury it in the backyard.' How the hell could a guy say this? I can think of a lot who might have said it.

"Contrary to that, the role of the priest is feminine. He's a caretaker, he loves everybody, he blesses all those people you don't like. Priests are men performing a feminine role. We finally got rid of the dress, you know, the cassock. But we call the church 'Holy Mother.'"

Run by the Holy Father?

Liturgy

Do you hear rumbles from downtown about your innovations?

"No rumbles," said Ben. "Not much innovation either. Inclusive language sometimes, as 'In the name of God our Creator, our Redeeming Brother,' etc., rather than 'Father, Son....' Or holding the host before communion, 'May you become what you receive' rather than 'Happy are those called to share in this supper.' Otherwise, I just strive to have a balance of men and women performers."

"Downtown is not the governor on liturgy changes," said Walt. "It's the people who get out of joint if you're radically different. At that point liturgy loses what power it might have.

"Rumbles come by way of the vicar, who calls to tell you about it, to reprimand or remonstrate or whatever he chooses to do. Our guy says, 'I got to tell you this, though I know you won't do anything about it.' We're talking little stuff, reported by quirky people who think it's their job to regulate liturgy. It's an odd mindset.

"So there's reporting and feedback, and nothing is ever done. I think that's fine. The system is just right on those issues. The limiting factor is my people as a whole, and that's how it should be."

Authority

Do priests have authority problems?

"I connect it with Psychology of the Priesthood, Number 18," said Walt. "Testing a priest, it would be good to put after his name how he deals with authority. Some feel good when doing the right thing, some when doing the opposite, some are sneaky. That's me. I consider myself sneaky. I don't want to confront, I don't want to be docile. I want to be sneaky, to do what I think is right and not ever make a case for it. I appreciate that some want to confront. I just don't want to be that kind of person."

Some find their happiness in going along with the church?

"Some are like that: 'My joy is to be a good boy,' " said Walt. "I just can't see it."

The Pope

"The pope read a condemnatory statement in Denver," said Walt. "He thought his presence there was to give this message. It was like Elvis thinking he had some philosophical truth to tell us. The pope doesn't get it. If he doesn't get it, why should anyone want to line himself up with him?"

"Authority people have to earn credibility today," said Ben. "I walk into a parish as pastor. The parish was there before me. There are all these relationships. People went to communion before I ever gave it to them. All this was going on. Then one day I show up.

"Now either I get in the stream of life so they can see I live their life, and only then do some leadership kinds of things, or I don't. But you have to earn respect, and the pope hasn't earned it. It's just 'I'm the pope and that's it.' He hasn't earned the right to be obeyed. If he had earned it, it would not come across as doing as you're told. It would come across as a leader leading us to a fuller life. That's something else."

"It is odd to see someone so out of it in that way," said Walt. "It's amazing that he's so popular, that he has this big influence."

"Who else gets a half million young people in one place?" asked Ben.

The Fantasy

In a hard-line church, "some would congregate in moral and doctrinal purity, and a lot would still go to mass and communion," said Ben. "But more would be turned away. People believe much more in God and Christ than in the priest and the church. Much more."

"It wouldn't make much difference," said Walt. "It's a matter of style, not of substance, and it's not all that important how you do it. But your own self-identity and satisfaction are another matter.

"If you go against your identity, you're in trouble. Take Tim, a priest friend of mine. He used to drink a lot. He was a wild man and funny. But he tore his guts out doing that. Now he's in a rigid mode. I like him now. He's still funny, though I wouldn't want to live with him or be in his parish.

"This new approach keeps Tim together, and I want him together. He does a lot of good. But if you asked the people in his parish if he's conservative or liberal, they wouldn't know what you were talking about.

"You have to be at the funerals and worry with people and the rest," Walt said. "Then you can do whatever you want."

Chapter 18

Fr. Tate:
Management by Meeting Needs

FR. ROBERT TATE, a pastor in a Midwestern city, treats his parishioners like customers. "And our customer is important to us," he said. "People come to us with needs. When they came to Jesus, he responded. He rejected only legalistic people.

"The law is not an end itself. It's to help us. As pastor, I can face toward the boss [the bishop] or toward my congregation. Here we face toward the congregation."

The congregation includes divorced, homosexual, and feminist members, many of them returned to the church ten or fifteen years after leaving in anger. "They found this a welcoming place," he said. "We doubled our numbers in the last three years. From around 250 attending all masses four or five years ago, we have grown to 600 attending just one of them. And that's in a church built for 450."

At the heart of this rejuvenation has been the parish's use of *The Deming Management Method,* a book by Mary Walton about management expert W. Edwards Deming, architect of the Japanese economic miracle. The book "seemed very Christian" to Fr. Tate. He read it and had his parish council and staff read it. They have been using it as a guide ever since.

This has meant setting up a parish structure geared to help people "function, be healed, build community." The financial structure, for instance, was changed so that the parish now gives one-third of its income to the poor.

Every year the council discusses whether to air condition the church, a $30,000-to-$40,000 job. "We discuss it and decide each time to give the money to the poor and remain hot."

The council also looked at what the church does that touches people's lives the most, which they decided was the weekend worship service. So they voted to spend another third of their income on that. That meant finding "the best choir director, actors, dancers, musicians, speakers, and sound system" and getting people to church by van or buying gas for volunteer drivers.

"That came from Deming. If you build quality, anticipate needs, and work at providing good experiences or at allowing the community to do so, then you don't worry about money. Money isn't our business anyway," said Fr. Tate.

"That simplifies a lot of questions, such as the conflict between a stated Vatican position and what happens in a lot of parishes. The people your book is about are those who tend to look toward the congregation," rather than to Rome.

He takes a graduate course every year, usually in theology or related matters, as in counseling, at a nearby Catholic university. He also does a lot of reading and thinking. Not many priests do, he has concluded from his experience giving priests' retreats around the country.

More than twenty years a priest, he feels such courses are needed. "In any profession, to operate with twenty-year-old information puts you twenty years behind."

Birth Control

Preparing couples for marriage, I bring up family planning. I say it's wrong to have more children than you can take care of and it's wrong to be selfish. How they do it covers a wide range. Some use natural family planning; others don't.

I say they should consider health and financial questions and how much time they will have for children if both are working. They should consider problems of world population. Some pieces are larger, some smaller in the pie. It's not just a simple right or wrong here.

Abortion

This parish has quite a few strong feminists, with whom I discuss abortion from time to time. It has pro-life people who take the "seamless garment" approach: they protest abortion, and they also address needs of children through an eighteen-parish Saul Alinsky–style community organizing effort. A number have gone to jail as war resisters. One-third of the parish income goes to the poor.

So we take a very strong stand for life, but on many fronts. I mention all these things in homilies, including abortion.

But as to whether to have an abortion, only a few times in twenty years have people asked, and then it's often a mother asking for her daughter. If after discussion a mother feels strongly that it's inappropriate, I urge sticking to her guns while remembering it's still her daughter she is dealing with. You don't just sit back and say nothing, I tell the mother. "On the other hand, neither do you throw your daughter out the door."

Marriage and Divorce

I run into bad marriages all the time. This parish is in a 90 percent black neighborhood. Many are converts, from other parts of the country. They come with no knowledge whatever of the Catholic prohibition of remarriage after divorce. The congregation has become two-thirds white, with the same number of blacks remaining.

The whites have a Catholic background and tradition. With them I try the annulment route. But in many cases there's no way to get evidence. A man married for two years, then divorced, comes in seventeen years later. He doesn't know where the former wife is. He's the only witness.

Or a couple married twenty years with children had earlier marriages that ended in divorce. Again, no case, but it seems the earlier marriages were not valid.

I have no problem with people deciding such cases for themselves. If the divorce and/or remarriage is recent, I counsel waiting a little. National statistics show 90 percent failure rate in second marriages within three years of divorce. Over that, even after only five years, the success rate is very high.

Altar Girls and Women

This parish has had altar girls for five or six years. Because it's interracial, issues of prejudice are quickly pointed out. So gender discrimination is an issue, which means girls serve mass and "God language" receives attention. It took me a while to develop appropriate language. The sisters educated me over the years.

The bishop, a wise and wonderful man with a Deming-like approach to leadership, didn't always agree with what was done. But if no scandal or outright sin was involved, he would let people work at what they chose.

There were no complaints and no problems about altar girls. If there had been complaints, there might have been a problem. But it was not a big issue for the bishop. He said that if he were asked officially, he would give an official answer. If not asked, he wouldn't. So don't ask, he said.

Women's ordination for us is a justice issue. I don't think Rome sees it that way. My parishioners see the church as a large, exploded model of the typical family, which means there are always things that need changing. But the church is worldwide, and it takes longer.

You work with it, you love it, you change it. You don't throw it out over one issue. Sometimes I apologize for our church. We've exploited a lot of people over the years, including many church employees — janitors, teachers, and the like. We just have to apologize and change the situation. It's that way with the women's issue. We are missing problems now that later we will recognize.

Gays and Lesbians

The parish has quite a few lesbian couples, I recently discovered. We start with the idea that everybody is important, and we run the parish to meet everybody's needs. Sexual orientation is secondary. We let it be known that all are welcome here and we have to work with each other.

Two years ago at a party, a black woman said that only whites can be prejudiced, and a big discussion followed. Later, in a homily, I called that notion "ridiculous" and said anyone can be prejudiced and we probably all are. It's part of the human condition. It's as prejudiced to say what the black woman said as to make sweeping statements about gays, Native Americans, or anyone else. Things like that come up from time to time.

Liturgy

The parish probably does little that could be considered unauthorized. We have variety and try to do it well. You might think you're in a Baptist church sometimes, because of the music and clapping. But at other services you might think you were somewhere else.

The gospel is always proclaimed, not read. Sometimes it's sung, sometimes acted out. The creed is not always the Nicene Creed, though strictly speaking we should use the Nicene. But we always have wine and bread, and we read the canon as it is in the book, though sometimes we elaborate and embellish it.

There is more drama and participation than, say, in Rome. It's not a passive event. That's one of the reasons for our dramatic growth.

The bishop has been here several times. Many priests come for mass, including teachers from our nearby university, who either sing in the choir or sit in the congregation. We also have a number of formerly active priests.

I am the only priest on staff, which also has a full-time sister as a pastoral minister and a half-time lay person who as committee organizer initiates and plans all sorts of things.

A parish is like a high school. You want each student involved in an extracurricular activity. So for our parishioners, we have study groups, sharing groups, social groups, youth groups, groups of old people, and others. We also have a small grade school, with almost all black students who are almost all non-Catholic.

The Pope

The general feeling in the congregation is that the pope has an important job and role, that there will always be a papacy. The problem is, the papacy is the last medieval structure in the modern world. As a structure it will go the way of the dinosaur.

This structure, with its top-down authority, doesn't work, especially in developed countries, with their high levels of education. People respect the office and the pope, but they don't take him seriously. Their focus is the local community, the parish. We don't worry too much about him.

From the pulpit I say I would do it differently if I had the pope's job. But I don't. Neither do I have his worldview. I see what he does from the vantage point of this community, where there's no acceptance of his structure.

As to his Denver appearance, the parish council decided not to send kids there, but instead to use the money locally for some retreat experiences for kids a day or two at a time. Ninety percent of the kids in our school are being raised by single parents on welfare. Only a few could have gone to Denver.

Liberal? Radical?

On a liberal-radical spectrum, I put myself in the middle, leaning toward the liberal, but not too far, because a group needs law for some kind of stability. The danger is that when one or other side prevails, the answer is either chaos or rigidity. Most of the congregation feels the same way.

Priests in general are more conservative than my parish and me, though they may do as I do pastorally. Some are more concerned with law-and-order issues and peer pressure. Abraham Maslow says most American adults operate from peer pressure and law-and-order motives, though some have universal concerns. My guess is the American priesthood fits that. In my travels around the country, I find examples of both.

Authority

I haven't had to employ subterfuge so far. I have felt free to disagree with my bishop, knowing he wouldn't take it personally. On some issues, he has had to invoke church teaching or take action when scandal was involved, as in removing a mentally ill priest or requiring another to undergo treatment for alcoholism or disciplining another for preaching scandalous things.

He has not been ineffectual. But as long as he could see some-one was working for the greater good, he was open to letting that happen. So we didn't have to play games. We could discuss things as adults. He didn't subject us to parent-child meet-ings. In a neighboring diocese, it's been much more oppressive. Priests have had to go their own way or go into game-playing — that or go before a firing squad.

A friend of mine worked up a template for the ideal corpo-rate vice president — one who takes directions and does not have his own agenda. On the template we put recently ap-pointed bishops. They were all raging vice presidents. They provide the pope a whole group to implement his agenda.

First, I was depressed to realize this. Then I realized that all it would take would be a pope of another color from John Paul II to turn things around. These bishops would all follow a new, more open pope as loyally as they do the present pope. And that may be what it takes to fully implement Vatican II.

It's not yet fully implemented. Only the theory has begun to take hold. Implementation would call for a more demanding church and a more collaborative structure. Clearly, the bishops at the council said, "We don't want the old church any more." But structures are hard to change. I'm not depressed about it. It takes a long time.

The Fantasy

A hard-line church in America would soon look like the church in Europe, because this is no longer an agrarian society, as it was even recently, and stability is no longer the highest value. Instead, it is an industrialized world, and mobility is the highest value.

Church and government once said, "This is how to do it," and that's how people did it. Look at the support for World War II. People no longer look to institutions, including the church, to learn what to do, but to have their needs met. If they find them met, they stay with the institution. If not, they say goodbye.

A few would have their needs met by a hard-line, almost fundamentalistic approach. But the vast majority would leave.

Obedience is important, but to whom or what? I say, to the gospel and its values. It jumps out at you: obedience not to structure but to a way of living, to God. Jesus' big conflict was with structure. He got the most grief from those stuck in it.

Chapter 19

Fr. Thatcher: The College Experience

F R. HENRY THATCHER, a religious order priest, is in parish
work after many years as a Newman chaplain on a state
campus. He gives a campus perspective on various pastoral
questions.

Birth Control

In my twenty years as a priest, birth control never came up,
partly because my clients have been mostly young and single
and partly because the sacrament of reconciliation is so little
used by students.

Abortion

An occasional student came to me, pregnant and in panic and
considering abortion but with much anxiety. I let her talk out
the anxiety. Together we explored alternatives. I never mentioned mortal sin, assuming that a Catholic coming to a priest
knows the Catholic position.

Others came after having an abortion, troubled about it. I
stressed mercy over God's judgment, trying not to imply they
had done anything unforgivable.

Where I hedge is, I never get into excommunication [as
provided in canon law], which provides no real assistance to
people. I deal with the person as needing reconciliation with
God, rather than legitimation by the church.

What has worked for me over time is that when someone

comes in with what they think is a sin, I never say it isn't but stress mercy and put what they have done in context. I make the point that it doesn't mean the person is a bad person. I try to communicate a strong sense of the mercy of God.

Large-university Newman Centers have become parishes for the alienated, especially in recent years. So even with a large staff, we tended not to touch abortion as an issue. There was not enough time to handle it from the pulpit, and in general it was an issue that generated more heat than light.

Burned by shouting matches between extremes in discussions, we settled on bringing in speakers who explored the issue in moderate, rational ways. We probably lacked courage to pursue it in other ways. I felt ill at ease with my silence. I was also reluctant to get up and spout off on it without enough time. I liked Archbishop Rembert Weakland's listening-session approach in Milwaukee. That's what's needed, people listening to each other.

I didn't (and now in a parish setting don't) deal at all with right-to-life people. I have had bad experiences with them. They're nuts.

Marriage and Divorce

At the Newman Center, we offered classes on annulment four times a year, and many came. I processed annulments for people who had had problems at their home parishes. I have found most tribunals pretty efficient and have always tried to go that route. The situation has improved considerably in the twenty years since I was ordained.

People who were refused annulment have asked me to perform a wedding anyway. I did that early in my priesthood but learned it was not a good idea. Often people did not feel good about it afterward (no better than I felt) and went to other priests with their regrets. So everyone was worse off than before. Besides, the Newman Center was a big and very public place, which led me to shy away from public ceremonies that were not kosher.

At the same time, I always distinguished between God and church, believing that being right with one is not necessarily being right with the other.

So my unannounced policy has been to refuse communion to no one, including the divorced and remarried. I have explored the question in conversation. When people decide it's important for their spiritual nourishment, I let it go, reasoning that God is for the hungry, not the well fed.

Altar Girls and Women

The server issue has not arisen, because I have never used servers, girl or boy. Women preachers are another question. Women staff members at the Newman Center preached regularly. It was reported to the bishop, who asked us to stop the practice.

This set off a round of negotiations with the diocesan liturgy office, whose non-negotiable requirement was that only the ordained proclaim the gospel. When preaching follows the gospel reading, it's considered part of the proclamation. So we moved the homily from gospel-proclamation time to before the gospel reading, whether men or women were preaching. The negotiations took six months, with give and take by both sides. The whole thing was a model of accommodation.

In addition, our staff developed an institute for lay preaching from which came the practice of lay people reflecting on the gospel passage at weekday masses.

We were fortunate to have a bishop who was not interested in hassling us. At the same time, he felt he had to do something about a clear violation of liturgical norms. It would have been different with another kind of bishop.

In fact, it was quite different in another diocese, where the bishop, well known as an upholder of church law, came on very aggressively in the women-preaching matter, forbidding it outright. His action shattered the community in question, also a Newman Center congregation. Some left and others felt alienated by what they considered authority coming from above, stopping something cherished in that community.

The residue remains from that action. There were other complicating factors, but that was the big one. It deflated a very Spirit-filled community, which had been performing a strong ministry to alienated persons in the area.

In our case, on the other hand, the attempt was made to consult everyone. The bishop could have said, "Don't do that," but he left us alone. Not that he was a free-thinker. He was theologically moderate-conservative but very pastoral. Being pastoral is what mattered.

Gays and Lesbians

The gay and lesbian question was a big item on the center's agenda. We offered a support group for gay Catholic men, not publicizing it but simply listing it among coming events. It was a low-key operation, but it was the only one of its kind in town, and the center became known everywhere as a church for gay Catholics. When a gay issue arose, like the Vatican's "Halloween statement" on homosexuality in 1986, local media called us, trying to set us over against the archdiocese. We tried to avoid that. We were working within the system. Our ministry was too important to jeopardize in that way.

Some wanted us to take a more vocal advocacy position, but I thought we should be as pastoral and mainstream as possible. So we cleared our events regularly with the diocese, telling them of speakers we were having and the like. We had to avoid public advocacy. Dignity [a national group virtually outlawed by the 1986 statement] engaged in advocacy and lost its legitimacy.

We presented it as a spiritual growth group for gay Catholics. We knew people came as couples but never called it a bad thing or told couples it was contrary to church teachings. People aired dissatisfaction with the church in meetings. The staff made church teaching clear but didn't push it down throats.

Couples wanted their relationships blessed. We performed no public ceremonies but did little things in this direction, such as house blessings. One or more of us would go to a couple's house and in a nuanced sort of way say, "God blesses you, this community supports you." It was a sort of back-door blessing of the relationship.

In all of this was a constant tension between supporting and affirming dedicated Catholics, some of the most committed we had, and remaining connected with the mainstream church. It was always a tightrope.

Liturgy

Inclusive language has been the main issue in recent years. A committee rewrote the readings, eliminating "father" for God except in the Lord's Prayer and instead using a traditional church term like "almighty God" or "loving God," or occasionally "O God, our loving mother and father."

Sometimes the committee changed the sign of the cross, to "In the name of the God who has created us, Jesus who redeemed us, and the Spirit who has made us one." Christmas carols and other traditional wordings they left alone, as they did what the people said together.

Some wanted "mother language" exclusively, but the staff felt that was setting out the red flag for more traditional people. There was tension between those who wanted much change and those who wanted none at all. Indeed, good people from both ends of the spectrum left the community over this issue.

Other things we did were not completely kosher, as not using the Nicene Creed, whose third-century language did not seem to fit. Recited in monotone, it produced a sort of drag in the liturgy.

The Pope

Priests of my era — formed by the '60s, given a relatively progressive seminary training, and experienced in working with students or alienated Catholics — have a more missionary approach than the pope. We try to make the church as welcoming as possible and experience discontent at the rigidity that the pope emphasizes. "Let's get the truths down hard and fast" is not our approach.

Still, the pope falls somewhere in between these two camps. He's a gifted man. I appreciate much that he has done, though I prefer the style of John XXIII and John Paul I [who reigned only a month, just before the present pope, John Paul II].

There is a good deal of mystery involved in faith. It can't be nailed down in hard-and-fast answers. It isn't as if there's a lucidity that can't be questioned.

I feel both discontent and discouragement. Twenty years ago, I was angry at things but expected to change them. Now I find there's not much one can do. I wish it were different. It's probably true of all popes. They are a mixed bag of hero and goat. That goes for most of us as well.

Liberal? Radical?

The romantic side of me would like to go with the alternative church. I remember the excitement of underground churches and of experimentation. But none of those lasted very long. And history shows splitting off leads to more splitting off.

The church is a gift, and there is something I cherish in the maintenance of unity and diversity. As painful as the struggle is, as toxic as it sometimes is, there is something healthy in it, because it forces us to deal with one another as part of one tradition.

I feel somewhere in the middle. The church is my family. It's what I was born to. It has given me much. Everything I believe that's true about reality can be found in the church.

My expression of it is Thomas Merton's expression, or John XXIII's. Merton's life incorporates all that I find of value in my tradition. There's tension here, because not all Catholics are like Thomas Merton or others whom I see as models.

Maybe that's a good thing. I struggle with it. Would it be better to go off and get all the progressive Catholics together and be free of legalistic hassle? I keep returning to the realization it wouldn't last very long.

Authority

I try to work with the system wherever possible, but I'm not averse to working outside it if I feel it's in the best interests of the people involved. It's a fine line. I have made mistakes on either side of the line. There are times when I followed the church and regretted it and times when I did something outside canon law and didn't feel good about it afterward. Other times, I responded to somebody and ignored or worked around church law because I thought it was the most pastoral thing to do, and I felt very comfortable about it.

It's my style to work within the system when possible, but some have another role, to be over against it, to be prophetic, and they do it very well. I take a stand if it's something I believe in. If we hadn't worked out the women-preaching problem at the Newman Center, I would have resigned my position there. I had spent too many years working with women ministers who felt strongly about their being excluded from public preaching.

I try not to defy the bishop, but I respond pastorally if I have to. I think that's pretty common.

The Fantasy

The hard-line approach is counterproductive. It legitimizes subterfuge and produces a schizophrenic situation. Currently we have much autonomy, though publicly we are limited. If we ever reach the point where pastors are forced to take a hard line, they will do as they always did: they will go underground, making their own accommodations.

Chapter 20

Fr. Burke
and the Sermon on the Mount

FR. JOHN BURKE, sixty-four, is pastor of Our Lady of Good Counsel parish, in West Boylston, Massachusetts, north of Worcester. "A priest of the '50s," as he calls himself (ordained in 1955), he makes much of the Sermon on the Mount. It's his litmus test, something he calls on to prove wisdom and recommend action. Asked if his name could be used, he chuckled. Asked if he defies his bishop, he also chuckled. He said yes to the first and no to the second, with the caveat given below.

Birth Control

When it comes up, I say very strongly that the union of the unitive aspect and the procreative aspect is basic in marriage. But as a pastor, I know people can't live up to it in a society like ours. It was probably different in an agricultural society. So I am understanding in that, but I do affirm the idea of it.

Where as a pastor I move away from official teaching is that I speak of it as an ideal, in a practical sense not to be achieved. The pope removed that cop-out, rejecting the notion of morality as unapproachable ideal. But the Sermon on the Mount does that. Jesus himself knew the Sermon on the Mount was reaching for the stars, not touching them.

The whole idea is it's a matter of attitude, of turning the other cheek, for instance. But how many have done that, lived

139

pacifism, which Jesus demands of us? Neither are we to judge others, but we can't pick someone up on the highway without judging. To be a Christian is to be striving. So it is with birth control.

As for receiving communion, we encourage one with hatred in his heart, who can't forgive, to do so. In the same way with those who practice birth control. You encourage going to communion.

Abortion

My anti-abortion ministry always exists as a category within the seamless garment. I don't preach on it, but on Jesus Christ, and include abortion as one of the struggles we have.

Marriage and Divorce

The priest must find where a couple is at. Priests tend if they are liberal to violate the conscience of people by pushing them into communion when they are not up to it. The priest should explain that with a good act of contrition and willingness to do penance, people must pick up where they are at and go forward. You encourage them to start where they're at.

I am amazed at the number of divorced people who say they don't believe in annulments. It's difficult to understand, because a lot go for it without thinking. But these take their marriage vows seriously and can't accept it. At least seven or eight of these I contact from time to time to say I'm there and to affirm the love of the church for them.

A man died recently, an organist, whose first marriage had been destroyed by his alcoholism. He recovered and married a woman who helped him recover. He served the church as organist but would not get an annulment. I would work with him and try to assure him. He was not in the state of what Augustine would call mortal sin.

Others I work with toward an annulment or in internal forum if they can't get one. I try to draw them closer to the Lord while respecting their ability to decide.

Altar Girls and Women

In a suburban parish, it's very hard to get servers. Kids are totally organized; the church is on the periphery. Three years ago, I thought, Maybe the girls will do it and opened serving to them. They would do it for six months or so, then resign because of other activity. The problem is not girls or boys. It's that children are sequestered from the church, except for mass and CCD, more than they would be under a totalitarian regime. It's hard for me, a priest of the '50s.

The question of women's ordination arises in a few church workers — very sharp, professional women, in management or medicine and the like. I tell them, if in time the Spirit of God guides the church to it, fine, but there is no possibility right now.

Also, we are in a period of great feminism. I think women should take advantage of this and seek more power in the church rather than ordination. Their frustration might interfere with their relationship with Jesus Christ and with what Jesus Christ has in mind for them.

A lot of the problem today is that we do not ask, What is the Lord asking of me right now, and What is viable? Is my call to ordination or to something else I don't have in mind? For context, I go back to the Sermon on the Mount, the bedrock on which we interpret anything.

In some dioceses, religious women have more power than priests. In the director of religious education position, you cede one-third to one-half of your ministry, you entrust it to a woman.

Gays and Lesbians

I was very involved in ecumenism in the '70s, including with the Metropolitan Church for gay and lesbian Christians. A former Catholic was running it. I was rector of cathedral at the time and brought them into the rectory. This ruffled some of the younger priests. You must talk to gays and lesbians and have compassion. Their condition seems to point to something in the genes, their DNA.

I encourage each to find someone to be a partner and loving

companion, as opposed to placing oneself in danger all the time by promiscuous behavior. It's a way least contrary to church teaching. Nothing is perfect. Perfection is to be compassionate. As for church teaching, I adhere to it. I also tell them of compassion and its basis, which is the Sermon on the Mount.

Liturgy

Every priest thinks he adheres to the way mass should be said. Is there a Burkeian rite? What does it mean? I see that over the years, it has changed. I haven't owned a cassock in years. I left it in a waste paper basket in St. Peter's sacristy in Rome. My bishop never wears one, though you're supposed to.

Do I do anything radical? The children's mass — I'm very free at that. I try to follow the guidelines, as in the loads of articles on how to preside in a fatherly way, not as from the chair of the Roman Caesars.

If I preside from the side of the altar, that's okay. Up there on the steps, in ornate surroundings, is that supposed to be fatherly? My church is long and hollow. So giving the greeting, I stand in front of the altar. I can't do it from the presidential chair in that church. In another church, like the cathedral, I could do it.

I keep in mind, What's the purpose of my actions? To be fatherly and familial. Even the term "presidential chair" takes from this. The liturgy expert Fr. Robert Hovda had great influence on me.

The Pope

Disloyal to the pope? No, I have profound respect for him. I agree with what Avery Dulles wrote in a recent issue of the London *Tablet* about his teachings on the dignity of the human person. It's remarkable, considering his origin, that he can touch the First World. He doesn't understand it, having grown up in the Second. Maybe he understands us better for that. It's good for someone to look at us, exhort us. I go for a lot of his emphasis on the dignity of the human person.

His latest encyclical, *Veritatis Splendor,* is not overly strict. There's nothing better than his encyclical on the Holy Spirit. I meditated on that for months. It was marvelous. The trouble is, many don't read his stuff.

About four years ago, a very hard, tough Unitarian who had retired from Harvard wrote of John Paul. He had got to know him in Krakow. He wrote how John Paul overwhelmingly quotes from the Book of Revelation. He's a visionary, a contemplative from the Carmelite tradition. There's a John of the Cross element in him.

But he's tough to read and follow. I read, then disagree, not in an intellectual but in a pastoral sense. A lot of priests don't read him, but howl at him instead. That's part of our problem.

Authority

I ignore my bishop to a large extent, carrying on in my parish. I was very involved with the previous bishop. Toward this bishop, one needs to be compassionate. We don't gel. I don't defy him. No circumstance has required it. I have criticized him publicly. Fraternal correction is required. I try to accept it myself; it's hard. He finds it very hard, because he's a very insecure man. He and I argue. I'm not one of his favorite characters.

He's gone through a lot with the pedophilia business. I've called him and told him I am praying for him. It's important when you disagree with a person to stay in contact, and to be as honest about yourself as about others.

Liberal? Radical?

We had a lot of that "idealism over all." We experimented with serendipity in religious education, the love syndrome, doing away with law. But Christianity is based on the flawed human nature we have. If it were not, there would be no redemption. Christians are not to put aside the law, which gives us discipline, but are to go beyond it. We need respect for the law. Matthew's Gospel brings that out strongly.

It dates from the Pastoral Institute at Loyola University in Chicago in the '60s, when there was a new director every year because the priest director married a nun. There was an awful turnover. It was all love and radical giving of the self. It left us without discipline and discipleship, which has to be challenged by the Sermon on the Mount to go further. Without discipline, we won't get beyond the law.

Today's catechesis teaches that the law is the way, that the law moves into the heart. First there's the external aspect, like what a child learns. The law set down by mother and father was a way of loving, we realize. One of the problems is we forget Paul's distinction between newly converted and others. The opposition of grace to law is a Lutheran concept, totally unscriptural. The first commandment is "I am the Lord thy God. Have no gods before me." It's false to say there was no grace in the Old Testament.

The Fantasy

Sean O'Faolain — or was it O'Casey? — quoted Edmund Burke, one of my heroes: "It is no small bit of wisdom to know how much evil is to be tolerated." The Irish priest, in Ireland, was good at it. I always come back to that. I have tried to live by that. Evil is everywhere, all intermixed.

Yet there are moments when I am rigid, like when I'm tired, on the phone. In my better moments, I try to live by that principle. A few things I am a stickler on and have to poke people to be aware sometimes — little rules, like who is to be a sponsor for confirmation. I expect a kid to choose someone ready to cooperate with me in ministry, an active Catholic. I don't insist on this with the baptismal sponsor, because that choice is caught up in family tradition. But Vatican II reconstituted the confirmation-sponsor idea, and I insist on that.

Chapter 21

Fr. Connole: No Monarchist, He

FR. MARLIN CONNOLE is a priest of the Seattle archdiocese based in the Seattle suburb of Bellevue. He was ordained in 1968, the *annus terribilis* of the '60s, when assassinations and riots tore the land.

His parish, Sacred Heart, is affluent, white, Republican, professional, full of physicians, lawyers, and executives, people for whom he says it is "innate to want things to remain as they are."

In the wars of the doctrines, he does meet vigilantes. His parish had a large contingent of people opposed to Archbishop Raymond Hunthausen, the anti-nuclear, liberal prelate who was subjected to early, forced retirement by the Vatican.

Remodeling his parish church was a "World War III experience" — a "springboard for dissent" from Vatican II. Conservative parishioners blocked the project for three years, sensing Vatican II–style changes in the offing. "They were right," he said. "We were embracing Vatican II and moving forward with it. We got through it, and now the church liturgically reflects the council. It was a very emotional thing."

He refers throughout to the mass usually as "the Eucharist." Asked if his name could be used, he said, "Yes. It cheapens the account if you don't."

Birth Control

It rarely comes up. I agree with Bishop Kenneth Untener's article in a recent *Commonweal*, where he said the *sensus fidelium*, the sense or consensus of the faithful, is part of the *magisterium*, or teaching authority. When this consensus is so out of sync with official teaching, as on birth control, do we have structures to listen and find out why? Not addressing questions like this makes us look like a dysfunctional family.

I said this in a Sunday homily and got all kinds of response, mostly positive. I said there's a difference between dissent and raising questions. We are a theological and not a fundamentalist church because we do raise questions, as opposed to Bible fundamentalists, who just form a new group when they disagree. Discussion, on the other hand, opens us to new awareness.

Priests need to read. How can they guide people otherwise? I was ordained in 1968, and the first new Vatican II liturgical rite was published in May 1969. I had to study that and many like it since then. One of the problems in the priesthood is that priests don't read enough.

Abortion

My contacts are more post-abortion than pre-abortion. I get the sense that women, and occasionally men, have a genuine struggle of conscience, before and after. Most make the best decision they think they can. I never found anyone for whom it was a simple alternative to birth control. Often it's a married Catholic woman who had an abortion in adolescence or one who had the abortion of a severely deformed child because her non-Catholic husband couldn't deal with it.

Everyone is in extreme camps, allowing no compromise. I liken the problem to the nuclear arms race, where the church reluctantly went along with building bombs. In our country, most agree abortion is not an alternative to birth control. But there are reasons people of otherwise like mind think it's okay, as in cases of rape. I have asked both of our bishops why the American bishops don't take a conciliatory approach. Why yes or no on this question, one or the other?

Marriage and Divorce

Our tribunal uses the annulment process to help people. Annulments are more available than twenty-five years ago, and lots use the process. Others just continue going to the sacraments after divorce and remarriage.

Altar Girls and Women

The bishop has been very tolerant of altar girls. From what I've heard, Rome is starting to rethink its position. It has become a non-issue. So many have them, more harm than good would be done if the prohibition were enforced.

The women question arises a lot. All you can do is encourage people to speak out with conviction. The bishops of northern Canada petitioned for married clergy. People just have to keep speaking on it.

Change under this pope? I don't see it. Rather, we are to be part of a church that excludes women's leadership. Women stay who were brought up with it, even if discontented. But younger women?

See Richard McBrien on what Rome can do in giving women power and authority. The heads of Vatican congregations need not be men. The pope can make women cardinals, who would vote for the next pope. On the local level, we can give women roles we now give to canon-law deadheads.

In a parish I served before this one, an older Catholic lady, the mother of nine, said of our parochial minister: "I don't care what the pope says, Patty Ribicoff is my pastor, and I will go to her for forgiveness."

The new code allows lay people to perform baptisms and officiate at marriages. A country's bishops must ask for it as a body. The American bishops asked and got it for Anchorage, where there was no priest. The fear is that by asking they acknowledge the problem. I'm the only priest for a fourteen-hundred-household parish. A nearby parish has one for twenty-six hundred households, and he is also a dean.

Gays and Lesbians

Our diocese has continued to offer pastoral ministry to gays and lesbians after Hunthausen's troubles, which stemmed partly from the diocese's gay and lesbian ministry. Dignity, the Catholic gay and lesbian group, can't function in any diocese. Our bishop has supported our active ministry. There's a Eucharist attended by gays and lesbians every Sunday evening at a parish, celebrated by different priests. One priest is liaison. Another heads the AIDS ministry. So there is pretty visible pastoral concern and expression.

I counsel four or five gays. Most of the struggle is to help them stay in the church. They feel excluded.

Liturgy

I do not use unauthorized innovations, but I believe the liturgy offers room for a lot of spontaneity. In the Eucharist, for instance, a priest may use the given or similar words in many places. For reconciliation there is no set form, so twice a year we have reconciliation services and bring to them a lot of creativity. Many parishes have general absolution. People are prayerfully moved by an hour together in a sense of brokenness and God's mercy and from this they experience more healing than from standing in line for a while for individual confession. Older people like it.

Parishes decide whether to give general absolution based on the number of people and confessors. Our problem is that we don't have enough priests. If there are four or five hundred people and two or three priests, we can't reasonably have individual confession. That's my understanding of why we have general absolution.

The Pope

The pope is certainly a strong presence. But his model won't work. He is not a bad person but sincere and committed to the faith. He comes out of a system where the church has something to fight, where the goal was survival under dictatorship. He feels that if he has more control, all will be fine. But this model will be hurtful for the church. I don't see it working.

He is not about to make an *ex cathedra* [infallible] statement. But people get confused, thinking his encyclical has the full weight of being infallible. I have talked at the Eucharist about dissent, recalling the case of Peter and Cornelius, of Peter being called back to explain himself to the other apostles. That's the collegial model, according to which he has responsibility to the other elders.

The papacy, on the other hand, employs a monarchical style developed in the Middle Ages. Papal infallibility further clouded the issue, so that many think all power is in the pope. At the time of our crisis here in Seattle, when Archbishop Hunthausen was under fire, the apostolic delegate, Pio Laghi, told us, "Remember, the bishop is vicar of Christ for your diocese, not a hired hand."

The bishop of Rome, the pope, has a preeminent role, but the model is the model of a king, with all else under him, so to speak hired by him to do what he wants. There was a struggle in Vatican II and under Paul VI to achieve more collegiality, with more power returned to the national bodies of bishops. John Paul II has reversed that, taking back to the papacy what belongs to bishops' bodies.

He has impacted the world with his visits. We can't fault him on that. But his model and his unwillingness to express people's concerns is not good, as shown in his refusal to meet with national bodies of women on his trips, such as the Leadership Conference of Religious Women or with gay Catholics. There is no outreach on his part; he doesn't say, "Let me listen."

Liberal? Radical?

The law is there to serve people. It can't be put above people and their needs. I always try to be clear about that when dealing with people in their various circumstances.

In the old days, people would ask permission to miss mass for a long Boy Scout hike. No eyebrows were raised at permission-giving. Or there was *epikeia*, which said not every law covers every circumstance. Or Bishop Butler's *sensus fidelium*, for when the moral law doesn't fit and people say it's time to find out why.

Striped lanes on the freeway help my driving, though nothing forces me to stay within them. There are times when I cross over, but I do it with caution. I even speed when I think I should. Of course, if I'm caught, explaining that to a state patrol person is not easy.

This is hard for many a Catholic to grasp. Many see church

law as if it were Anglo-Saxon law. But church law follows the Roman model, as in most of Europe. Can the Anglo-Saxon approach be a problem here? Absolutely. All kinds of things mitigate the offense. We are not real good at seeing mitigating factors.

Authority

I never had to do employ subterfuge or defy my bishop. People write the bishop and apostolic delegate when they are upset with me, as they did during the church remodeling process. What I do, I stand up for and take the consequences. I can't think of anything I would do in defiance.

The Fantasy

I would leave the ministry before I would work in a hard-line church. It would not be my idea of a healthy church, and I couldn't do it. How widespread would that reaction be? I can't tell you. But that's my bottom line.

Genuine pastoral care is one of the benefits of Vatican II that I can't sacrifice. That kind of church is not something I would support with my gifts and talents. I would like to think others would react the same way. But with push coming to shove, with job loss involved, and the like, I can't be sure. But I don't see that happening.

Chapter 22

Fr. Edgeworth: No Mincer of Words

FR. ED EDGEWORTH was a military chaplain for many years. Now, over thirty-five years a priest, he heads a big suburban parish of small, neat homes. He was clipped and to the point in a telephone interview.

Birth Control

People don't ask. If they did ask, I'd say it's a probable opinion that they can practice birth control and be a faithful member of the church. People are going to follow their own conscience on this.

Abortion

Abortion is wrong, but I'm no zealot. I put fillers in the bulletin, like one saying, "It's your choice to have a life but you should never kill someone to have a choice." Nobody has asked, saying, "I want one, can I?"

The parish sold raffle tickets recently for Courage, which offers an option to abortion. We announced it as helping unwed mothers, etc. That's the approach we should take, telling about adoption, etc.

Marriage and Divorce

I usually send people through the annulment process, especially if they have time. Every once in a while, someone ignorant of the requirements wants to get married. One was married in the Navy in the Philippines, it lasted six months, it was blatantly not a valid marriage, they don't even know the difference. I skip it then and use internal forum. If they think they need the process, I go through it.

Altar Girls and Women

We have altar girls. Only a few don't. I'm really surprised when someone says it's wrong. It shocks me, as the conservative couple who say they are moving because of this and other things. These are CUF people [Catholics United for the Faith, a conservative group], and it happens very seldom. Most are very happy about it.

Do I discuss it with the bishop? No. As pastor of the parish, it's my responsibility. It's not an issue.

The women question arises, yes. I pray to "God our father and mother" before the Prayers of the Faithful. We have women lectors, women ministers of the Eucharist, and the rest. If someone asks about ordination, I say I have no control over that. For the weekly Stations of the Cross this year during Lent, we had women leading it. One would lead the prayers, others went station to station with a candle, dressed in choir robes. Once it was three women, but usually it was two men and a woman or some other combination.

Gays and Lesbians

Gay and lesbian issues don't arise at all.

Liturgy

We have the confessional service, with readings, song, and prayer. People come forward and we place hands on heads. If they want to say their sins, they can. Then we give absolution to the group. It's no problem. It's not bothering me at all.

The Pope

The pope is a fine man, but he has nothing to do with our parish. He's a figurehead, a symbol of unity for the church. He is the principal theologian of the Catholic Church but not the only one. We must listen to him and give consideration to what he says, but he's not the final word.

Most priests I'm in contact with say the same thing. They are more concerned about paying off the mortgage than reading the latest encyclical.

Liberal? Radical?

A lot of religious get carried away. We have to preach the gospel, and there's a radical element to it, but without laws it's anarchy. If we are to be a church, we have to have rules. A certain pastoral prudence is to be used.

Authority

I'm not burdened by the bishop's authority. Ours is a good man and a reasonable man. I once told him he's a lousy preacher, that while he's reading his sermon, I tune him out. He listened. There are some who wouldn't.

The Fantasy

If there were no bending, we would lose everyone under fifty. The white heads would not be happy but would continue till death. And that's how the church would go. It would be thirty years at most before nobody was left.

Chapter 23

Fr. Gaunt: The Joys of Counseling

F R. JERRY GAUNT was ordained in the late '60s in a Midwestern diocese. He was one of a group of young priests
who exuded a spirit of fraternity while more or less protesting
various situations, including an intractable bishop. A smiling,
friendly man, he heads a mostly black parish. He concentrated
on two issues, abortion and marriage-and-divorce, weighing
and balancing them like a jeweler with a stone.

Abortion

I marched against abortion once, carrying a sign that said, "Unborn women have rights too." I'm still moved by that. I read
somewhere that when abortion is based on gender, the female
child is aborted 80 percent or so of the time.

A woman came to me once, spilling her troubles and down
on herself in general. "The Smiths are losers," she said, referring
to herself and her family. Four years later, she came back saying
she was doing much better, but was now pregnant though unmarried and was considering an abortion. The father was her
boss. It seemed she was giving herself another reason to start
hating herself again.

At the time I was hearing confessions at a nearby hospital,
where I had lunch one day with a staff psychologist, a woman.
I told her about this Smith woman, adding that in my non-
directive way I had avoided imposing my ideas on her. She said
I might have erred in that. Smith could have gone to a non-

priest for that much. Maybe she wanted someone to tell her, absolutely, "Don't do it."

Women have come to me in and out of confession years after their abortion, some depressed on the anniversary of the abortion or of the birth that never happened. One woman had trouble distinguishing between her present baby and the one she had aborted.

Another I met at a hospital where I had gone to give last rites to her mother. She pulled me aside to talk about her abortion, and when others of the family interrupted, she told them to "get the hell out of here" while she talked to me, so intent was she on getting her story out. I had never met her before.

Marriage and Divorce

The church can't grant an annulment until the parties are divorced. The person must go out on a limb, get divorced, and only then see if there's any annulment possibility. So it's the person's decision to get divorced, and only later the church ratifies that or not, deciding whether there was Christian grounds for doing so.

People have to understand what the church is saying — not that the first marriage no longer exists, but that something of Christ was missing that would have bound the couple together for life.

People know there was a marriage. There just wasn't enough of Christ in it to make it for life. The average lay person does not believe it never existed, unless a son or daughter was married to someone they knew from the start was nuts, and thus incapable of marriage.

Some worry that annulment makes children illegitimate. The typical answer is no, because the annulment has no civil effects, and that's a civil question.

Some get divorced frivolously. But even that is a sign something is missing. My bias is that everyone gets a divorce for good reasons; so there's probably an excellent chance for annulment. People don't get divorced over nothing.

Observers say things were going fine for the first few years, then the husband began running around. Even if it took a few years, that's a sign he was never too serious about stability.

From the pulpit, I say that in the annulled marriage something serious was missing and I give examples. At the end of this sermon, I turn figuratively to the young unmarried in the congregation and say, "So be very careful whom you hook up with. You may think you're in love, but five years later the church may look at it and say that was such a goofy character you married, that the marriage can certainly be annulled." I turn the discussion into a warning to young people.

After marrying many people in twenty-six years as a priest, most of them in the more Protestant-oriented African-American community, I preach on the subject once a year.

A priest I know solved the already-married convert problem this way: When they asked to be married in the church, he told them, "In the Catholic Church, you can only get married once," making it sound like a technicality, and sent them to the County Building. They would go downtown, get married civilly, and return to parish life not realizing they had a problem.

I don't endorse the practice, but I find it interesting. It's good that he didn't lay a guilt trip on them, but their innocent ignorance won't last. Sooner or later, they will hear from other Catholics that their status isn't legal. "You don't go to communion now, do you?" they will be asked, and will forever after wonder where they stand as Catholics.

The priest owes them an explanation. They should come in with the friends who questioned their situation. The priest can play good cop and bad cop.

The friends will be legalistic about it. To the strict ones, he can say, "What about the Lord's message of understanding and not bending the bruised reed?" To those pleading freedom in all things, he can say, "What about the church's tradition on marriage? You can't just throw that out."

From the discussion can come deeper understanding. The people involved will have more than a priest's reaction on which to base their decision. They will understand how the Lord looks on stuff like this and can be at peace about it, no matter who challenges them.

I do this regularly. I work with people until they weigh everything and come to a workable conclusion.

A couple came to see me once, full of confusion. George and Julie, let's say. George had been married. He had applied for annulment. But he didn't want to wait for it before marrying Julie. Julie and her family wanted to wait. Every time she would start to give in, he would say, "Are you sure?" And every time he would agree to wait, she'd say the same thing to him.

They finished their discussions in July. When they walked out of the last one, I was sure they'd be married in a month. At Thanksgiving I heard from Julie, full of gratitude for my help and telling me, "I think you knew at the time that George and I were drifting apart." She thought I had read the situation correctly. But I hadn't. It was the end game, but it had gone right past me.

Chapter 24

Fr. Irwin:
A Black-Community Experience

F<small>R.</small> C<small>AL</small> I<small>RWIN</small> heads a small black inner-city parish that averages 240 people at Sunday masses. An order priest, he has worked in the African-American community all his twenty-some years as a priest. His comments reflect that experience.

Birth Control

In the black community, birth control is of more recent concern, especially in the public housing community. Most women had children when they were young. By the time they got to where they were responsible, they were raising others' children, doing the godlike thing.

In this parish women want children. Only after three or four do they consider birth control. They are not thinking of an extra car or TV set. They have done what God asked of them and have a full-time job raising their children. They are fairly confident of their decisions. In any event, I don't make decisions for them.

Abortion

I have no conscious abortion or anti-abortion ministry. For the most part, African-American women are against abortion. The stigma in having children out of wedlock is not as great. Pregnant women are encouraged by their families, who offer help, though a rebellion is growing among grandparents, who are less willing to raise their children's kids.

I've never met a priest who openly advocated abortion.

Marriage and Divorce

Two of our holiest people are in a bad marriage, the second marriage for both. They have found God and are coming to church. I go by how they are living right now. If they are in a committed, loving relationship, that's of the Holy Spirit. If the signs are there, the fruits of the Spirit, I have to conclude the Spirit is there.

They are the head of our liturgy committee and the head of our Eucharistic ministers. They bring elderly to church. When a family was burned out, they sent money anonymously. I knew they did it; the recipients didn't. Both have good jobs and make good money. I'm sure they give half of it away. If I were looking for a married couple to canonize, they would be it. Both are very grateful for each other. His eyes water at talk of their love. God has to be in that marriage.

I don't want to universalize from that. I would not say from the pulpit, "Get divorced and remarry; you might do better than now." That's crazy. I take what comes. Some say, "This marriage is destroying me." I say, "Maybe you don't belong in it." I am much stronger on helping the individual than on saving marriage as an institution, though I respect the institution.

Gays and Lesbians

I wouldn't bring it up with someone, even if I knew he or she was gay or lesbian. I'm not confrontational. My criterion is what kind of person you are. Greedy, exploitative, selfish, ungodlike? Or one who loves too much and strikes a balance that is off center in the church's view? The church needs passionate people.

Liturgy

Where I was pastor in another city, our liturgical dance group was scheduled to perform at a diocesan African-American Day program. The bishop called me and said, "Do not dance in my cathedral." We changed it to "offertory procession with movement and gesture," and when he saw it, he loved it. I'm not beyond saying the words they want to hear.

We have passion plays with dancing here. If you're going to read the Magnificat [Mary's song, "My soul doth magnify the Lord"], you might as well dance it. Was it unauthorized? I never asked anybody.

We have an excellent gospel choir and do a little shouting and clapping that might not be appreciated in other churches.

We do not silence women who want to say something. They give "reflections," not homilies. Many are better preachers than I. And we have witnessing during mass or during announcements at the end. People get up to thank the parish for assistance received, and it turns into a second homily.

The Pope

I don't feel disloyal to the pope. I respect him for what he's trying to do. And I certainly would not want his job. The positive things he says are very good. If he could just keep giving us inspiration and general principles, it would be fine. I like him a lot more than I dislike him, though I don't feel like giving up my intellect and will. At parish staff meetings, we criticize each other, but we still love each other.

Liberal? Radical?

I respect the law but don't apply it rigidly. It's a much needed guide, but a lot of cultural and social adaptations can't be written into it.

Authority

I consider myself obedient — to the bishops, my religious superiors, the government, others in my community. It's a bit broader than straight from the top. I don't defy bishops and I don't live in fear, but I do exercise prudence. This bishop is pretty good. It's not a burning issue here.

The Fantasy

The church belongs to the less than perfect people of the world. We say "Lord have mercy" at the start of each mass. We'd have to delete half of Scripture if we were all perfect to start with.

The perfect church is an illusion. It's not real. I would hate to see a hard-line church. I would fear it more than anything else I can think of. It would drive away those we need the most, those who need and have experienced and give mercy.

Chapter 25

Fr. Cudmore: Radical with Jesus

F**R. MATT CUDMORE** has worked largely in Spanish-speaking parishes in his almost twenty years as a priest in a Midwestern diocese.

Birth Control

I present the church's teaching as an ideal. It's where we start. When someone asks about it, I figure that person is *ipso facto* a responsible person. I try to help them evaluate their situation as to number of kids, economic circumstances, and the rest, encouraging them not to be afraid to make a responsible decision. That's as a counselor. I never preach about it.

Abortion

Again, the church's teaching is where we start. It's the ideal. I have never been asked about abortion before the fact, but Hispanic women come frequently in confession after having an abortion, carrying tremendous guilt. Most of the aborted pregnancies I hear of occur to an unmarried woman after a night of passion. I try to make them feel forgiven and worthy, applying a ministry of healing.

Strictly speaking, I should refer penitents to the bishop for lifting the excommunication they incur by getting an abortion, or I should at least apply to the bishop on their behalf. But I let them confess and be forgiven on the spot.

Marriage and Divorce

I run into bad marriages very frequently, especially at first communion time, when parents want to receive communion with their children. The parents explain their situation. We sit and go over their history, finding very often that the previous marriage was a non-marriage, with a lot of violence or alcoholism.

I ask the couple if anyone would be scandalized by their receiving communion. If so, I discourage them from doing so. But this is rare, because most of them are not known to be previously married. If the partners are faithful to each other and intend to form a Christian home, I say they should consider themselves in a good marriage and should receive communion.

I also say they should start the annulment process. But this is difficult for the Hispanic people I serve, because it's in writing and theirs is an oral culture. The questions are difficult even when translated for them. The whole process ignores their cultural situation.

Altar Girls and Women

This parish has altar girls. Everybody has them. I have never discussed it with my bishop, who has seen the girls and said nothing about them.

The women question arises very often, especially among women on the parish staff — the nun who is a pastoral associate, for instance, and the wife of our permanent deacon.

I tell them it's part of a historical process that will take time. Everybody has to be patient, I tell them. Radical change such as ordaining women is difficult for the majority of Catholics, and we must go slow or we lose them, I say. People are open to new things, but there must be a process. The church is only two thousand years old, which is young compared to some other world religions. It is still more or less in its adolescence. The women are not moved by these arguments.

Gays and Lesbians

I am more sympathetic to the gay and lesbian plight, partly because my brother, a gay man, died recently of AIDS, at home,

with all of us around him. Every once in a while, a gay or lesbian comes for confession or spiritual advice, which I try to give
in a spirit of reconciling and healing.

Liturgy

I have given general absolution in a communal reconciliation
service attended by four hundred or more people with only
two priests present. As in the Cursillo [a retreat program of
Hispanic origin], I have had people write sins on pieces of paper, then burn the paper in a small fire at the front of the
church. This supplied the symbolic action that satisfied the
individual-experience requirement.

I aim at complete gender inclusivity at mass, changing the
words of the canon where necessary. Women have preached at
homily time. We don't call it a homily but a reflection. That's
how we get around it.

The Pope

The pope is doing the best he can, fulfilling his role as center of
unity for the church. I admire how he goes out visiting. I do not
feel disloyal to him.

He's criticized for his conservatism, but we must consider
where he's from. He really doesn't know any other reality than
Poland. Some of his own writings are very powerful. It's a side
of the pope that many don't realize, a prophetic side, as in his
criticizing the non-freedoms in our value system, among them
consumerism. He hits on that a lot, and I respect him for it.

Liberal? Radical?

It's not a question of liberal or radical but of being committed to
the gospel and seeing the world through the eyes of Jesus.

Sometimes you have to challenge people, sometimes be
forgiving. The gospel sets the parameters for one's response,
including never to make a situation absolute.

A lot of Catholics want to see things in black and white.
But Jesus was constantly breaking the law. The woman caught
in adultery should have been stoned, if the law were to be

followed, but Jesus forgave her. King David ate temple bread, normally off limits, and fed his soldiers because they were on the run and hungry. He was definitely breaking the law.

Jesus' action in this case was incredible. The same with the blind man in the temple, whose eyes he opened, refusing to blame his parents for his being born that way. In this he challenged a basic Jewish belief. Jesus was supposed to find someone to blame but wouldn't.

The Pharisees checked with the man's parents to be sure he had been born blind. The blind man was thrown out of the synagogue because he insisted Jesus had cured him. Jesus was acting in very radical fashion, attacking the law of Moses.

He did this in the temple, the heart and soul of Jewish life, to reclaim it for God, take it back from the Pharisees and high priests. We don't realize how radical Jesus was.

At issue is whether the church serves or is the kingdom of God. If you think it is the kingdom, you will be obedient in all things. But I believe it only serves the kingdom, and from that comes my understanding of the role of authority, namely, to free people to love God and each other.

The passage in Matthew 25 is crucial, where the saved are identified by whether they welcomed Jesus in the poor and the hungry. This is authority for me.

The Fantasy

Would churchgoing plummet in the wake of a hard line? Definitely. Consider what I say here. The average Catholic would not be shocked by what I have said, only the more traditional ones. When I started out, I held the line on everything. But as I matured in the priesthood, spending time with many good priests, mostly in the inner city, my parameters widened.

I have grown, I think, in my ability to listen well and apply the gospel. The gospel is a source of energy for me. I love the Scriptures. I live in that world and try to see life through the Scriptures. I also love the church. I take things seriously. It has been a fulfilling life.

Chapter 26

Fr. Eaton:
Two Laws, Canon and Pastoral

F R. TOM EATON heads a small-town but growing Midwestern parish near a major tollway. He's over thirty years a priest, twenty years a pastor. His parish, where he arrived recently from serving a city parish, is registering new families at the rate of more than one a day. "In none of this," he said at the end of the interview, "do I consider myself a maverick."

Birth Control

It doesn't come up, and we don't bring it up. We promote mutual love, not don'ts for the intimate life of the bedroom.

Abortion

We have a strong pro-life committee. At a former parish, we ran a crisis pregnancy center. Thousands of girls came each year for pregnancy tests, food, clothes for girl and baby, expense money — all in hopes that the girl would keep the baby. We take a strong pro-life stance. Priests do, in my experience.

Marriage and Divorce

I take couples through the annulment process. It's probably more important for them to get a piece of paper from the institutional church saying they are free to marry than it is to have a priest say, "Don't worry about it."

When nothing can be done, the internal forum can and should be used after deliberating with the couple, so they understand, assuming they are not just angry or impatient.

There is pastoral power and canonical power. As a shepherd, working with people, I see their hurt and pain. Sometimes law and pastoral office conflict. When I follow another law, of charity, I am not disobeying the first law. There are times when I am obligated to set aside canon law for the internal forum.

Some priests won't do it, to protect themselves or because they think it's against the law. They think canon law is the only law there is. I don't do it every week, more like once a year. I don't give out annulments with ease, as some priests do. But I do what I can for the good of the people.

Where did I get these ideas? From working with people. You have the obligation as pastor to meet people's needs. They came from my experience.

Altar Girls and Women

I started girl servers in my previous church. It worked out real well. Women should be involved in our church as much as men. We really haven't come of age. I have women pastoral ministers, and otherwise we are doing all we are permitted to do. The only other thing is to state your opinion openly and hold your ground. Jesus wasn't saying women couldn't be priests.

Gays and Lesbians

I feel insecure about gay and lesbian issues. I have counseled only one or two gays. I felt sorry for them. They were trying to be good persons. But I also felt ineffective, almost not knowing how to deal with them. My "do your best" was pretty generic advice. I don't know if it's sufficient. I think if two men or two women live together and are not promiscuous, they need and should have the sacraments.

Liturgy

Do I bend the law here? I don't think so. There's enough you can do without bending it, like creative use of Penitential Service 2 in the code. I've seen it done and found it devout and not disrespectful. It would be wonderful if we all could do it. I mentioned it to my bishop, but he said no. He thought it was not a good idea.

The Pope

I swing from calling him a disaster to saying, "This is a real pope." I think he's quite good in his liberal statements on social justice. But he's not a new kid on the block and should know what will be reported. Why not come in, be charismatic, be a radiation of papacy, use the power of his person, without getting into statements as he does? He thinks he will carry the ball himself. He won't, he can't. He seems not the pope for the hour.

He should take a broader view, less Eastern European. He combated communism, and for that he is a hero. But he does not seem to have a grasp for a society such as ours struggling with its problems. Has the Western world rejected Christianity, as he seems to think? Many have not. I wish the pope would address himself to prayerful people, who need encouragement.

It's disappointing when he gets harsh, talking to millions. This becomes the image of the Catholic Church. He would attract more people with a different approach, saying they would like to be on his team. He has nice charisma, if he would let it be.

Liberal? Radical?

My attitude to the law? In my new parish, I find myself borderline shocked to see so much disrespect for the law, as in worship matters. People are so easy on themselves, claiming they can't make it to church. How easily we do away with the law. I don't respect that laxity.

We must be prayerful people. It's our anchor. I am not happy to hear a young couple say, "We are so busy doing good. If we can't get to mass, God will understand." This is baloney. It discards the whole vertical message of the gospel. Maybe there are a lot of immature and unsophisticated people today, from any kind of school, Catholic or not.

Authority

Authority from the bishop is not a threat, nor is there fear of recrimination. Nor — almost — do I care. I try to cooperate because the bishop has a tough job. At the same time, I have an obligation to people in the parish, so that if I think something is for the birds, I certainly won't go ahead with it.

Nor do I practice strict adherence to what he says. The people feel the same way. It doesn't mean we don't like him, but the day of princes is over, and has been for a long time.

We live in the local church — the parish church. People who like their parish are happy with the church. As for statements of pope and bishops, people don't care one way or another. They have enough problems.

We do not worry what someone thinks in the see city [where the bishop resides]. Most priests care only from their desire to cooperate, and certainly not from fear.

We will have a new bishop soon. There could be a problem. New bishops are being made today from a list of people who never objected to anything.

The Fantasy

The church would just dry up. The old ones would go along. They have one foot in heaven already. But young adults would politely say, "God bless you and goodbye." They wouldn't fight or insult you. They would just leave.

Pastoral sensitivity and leadership is necessary, and people want it. Real leadership is not that the priest is a wimp but that he works in the context of parish councils, etc. He has to show leadership and promote it among lay people.

We live in a world that respects competency in a priest. Just being ordained doesn't get him a free pass.

Chapter 27

Fr. O'Connell:
A Pastor-Canonist Comments

FR. PAUL O'CONNELL is an ex-*officialis*, that is, he once sat on the marriage tribunal of his diocese of Worcester, Mass. This was after post-graduate studies in canon law at Catholic University of America, immediately after Vatican Council II.

He recalls the post-council period as "a great time, with so many changes." He commends the Canon Law Society of America for its "much good work against great odds," including research on women's ordination and mandatory celibacy for priests.

He is currently pastor of St. Mary's church, in Shrewsbury, Mass., an upper-middle-class congregation.

Birth Control

I usually raise the issue during marriage-preparation sessions, in pre-marriage inventories. I give the church's official position and say why natural family planning might be a good option.

I say it doesn't work well for all, however, and calls for input from a good moralist and a doctor. It's responsible parenthood, rather than birth control, I say, though natural family planning is a form of birth control. A lot of couples are interested in natural things, such as natural family planning, for which timing is all, rather than chemical or other intervention.

Abortion

I can count on two hands the number who asked about it in my thirty-three years as a priest. They know what a priest would say. They know the official position. But they make up their own minds. In the few cases that have come to me, it's been delicate. Some have been told the fetus is not viable, that it's handicapped, and the like. It's not just "I don't want to have a baby." You run into some heavy stuff there.

The Rachel ministry is available for those who have had an abortion and want to talk about it.

This parish has a big pro-life group, especially among doctors. It does the usual things — selling red roses, marching, giving out information. Its members will probably be over at the new abortion office in town, demonstrating a bit, though they won't block entrances. And there's a diocesan group. I'm not much involved in these activities, but I permit them.

Marriage and Divorce

A parish like this has a lot of bad marriages. A lot in their second marriages are very active, especially if there are children. If I find out about it or am in touch with them, I raise the idea of going to the public forum, and then, if that doesn't work, to the internal forum, at least in terms of the sacraments.

I push the public forum, having worked in it a long time myself and knowing its therapeutic value. If it's done right, it can have pastoral value. Some just go their way. I leave them in good faith.

Altar Girls and Women

We have altar girls. Our bishop suggests it's a silly issue and turns the other way, more or less saying, "Don't ask me." If a newspaper called me about it, I would call them "sanctuary helpers," giving them another name. If the bishop is questioned publicly, he states the official position. But he won't press pastors to stop it.

There's very little push around here for women's ordination. At a general parish meeting recently, it was suggested to enhance the role of women in the church. There are so many things women can do by way of decision-making in the parish — as director of religious education, youth minister, school principal, or parish council head, to name a few. We have shared ministry and a good staff with joint decision-making. In that sense women obviously play a role.

Three or four times a year, women give spiritual reflections during mass at homily time.

Gays and Lesbians

The diocese has a ministry to gays and lesbians and an AIDS project. In personal counseling, as often in my tribunal work, where it came up as grounds for nullity, I have tried to explain the church's position, saying the person may not agree. I never went much beyond that. At the tribunal, the partner with the gay orientation would come in and chat. Some priests have married gay couples and have been called in to the chancery for that. I wouldn't do that.

Liturgy

The only unauthorized thing I do is a reconciliation service. Several options are allowed, but a lot of priests give general absolution, which is not really approved by the bishops but is included in the code of canon law. The new Ritual [the book of approved liturgical services] has room for communal penance, as in large crowds, etc. The question is, how large?

Most say individual weekly confession is dead. People come for communal confessions, especially in Lent or when kids are making their first confession. Then the whole family comes out.

The time of first confession — whether before or after first communion — is left to parents. We teach them all in second grade. In fact, the next first-penance group consists of kids from second through seventh grade.

The Pope

Most people respect the pope and the office. This one they respect a great deal without agreeing with him, not even on social justice issues. Some priests think he's out to lunch. But most recognize his commitment and convictions.

I don't feel disloyal to him when I disagree on some things. The office of Rome brings people together. It's the only place in the world where people can come from all over and feel an identity. There has always been dissent in the church.

Most dissent in recent years has been over his reluctance to grant laicizations to resigned priests, permitting them to marry. Those who apply for it are the ones who want to remain in the church. They are the ones who get hurt the most.

Liberal? Radical?

It's an interesting question. I'm on the side of the progressive. I tend to accept change and growth, rather than stay with tradition. A lot of younger clergy are more conservative, maybe in reaction to the liberalism of the council, especially on some liturgical issues.

I was in Ireland last week, out in the boondocks, without television. I read the Bible, St. Paul. So often he talks of the biggest sin being legalism. In St. Paul and in the gospel too, it's "Let the spirit work."

Authority

Some use subterfuge in handling marriage cases. I have altar girls, which is a very public thing. A lot depends on who the bishop is. Sometimes a pastor can exercise discretion in a parish, as a bishop can in a diocese, as in whether godparents are confirmed or not. This is something pastors can decide. A lot of priests aren't aware of the discretion that's open to them.

We are very blessed here with our bishops. Bishop Flanagan was a great guy, a canon lawyer. Bishop Harrington is a kind of humanist. He thinks with his heart rather than his head.

The Fantasy

If with the hard line there was compassion, a sense of understanding, people would not leave the church. Those who leave it around here are looking for more spirituality, a more intimate sharing of faith, as in a new pentecostal group, Triumphant Life Ministries. Not a lot are leaving because of abortion or birth control.

Another thing that pushes people out is this: If they have no voice, they go elsewhere. They leave for a positive thing, not for a negation. They can ignore the negation. Marriage law is a big source of leakage, but if people really want the church, they can rise above this. You see any number of twice-married at mass with their kids on Sunday.

Chapter 28

Fr. Smith: A Reluctant Critic

F R. JAMES T. SMITH is pastor of St. Matthias Church, a twelve-
hundred-family, working- and middle-class parish in Co-
lumbus, Ohio. It's a pleasant neighborhood, with many Italian-
Americans already part of it and some Southeast Asian and
African-American families moving in.

Fr. Smith has been a priest for twenty-nine years, all of them
spent in parish work. He has been willing in the past to "stick
his neck out," as a friend put it, on one occasion seeking to
gain priests' senate support for a disciplined theologian, the
Dominican Matthew Fox.

Birth Control

It rarely comes up. When it does, I give the official teaching, saying most people have trouble with that and they should do the
best they can in life.

Abortion

It rarely comes up. When it does, I'm clear on what the church
teaches and on my agreement with it. Unlike with birth control,
I present no leeway.

Marriage and Divorce

I run into more marriage cases than I can handle. The church
should get out of the tribunal business. But since it's in it,

people have a right to use it. They have a right to get out of the bad marriage. I help with the process, but only for two or three cases a year.

Altar Girls and Women

I have had altar girls in my last three parishes, over the last fifteen years. I have never discussed it with my bishop, who I guess has decided not to fight the issue, though he doesn't particularly like girl servers. I also guess that one-third of our parishes have them. The bishop can't fight something so widespread. The ruling will change anyway.

As for the women question, I consider it an injustice that they are not ordained, and I bring the matter up now and then. It's also a loss to the church. But the issue does not arise in my day-to-day ministry.

Gays and Lesbians

It's a non-issue in my practice of the ministry.

Liturgy

I do not employ unauthorized innovations. Some find the liturgy not gripping or dramatic or engaging enough. It's a heady experience to substitute something they think is better. But what has been devised to make it better has largely failed, from what I have heard. Innovations have been largely sloppy and sentimental. People don't know how to make it better.

Liturgy is for the most part well constructed and has a power of its own that we ought to respect. If we priests prayed the liturgy as it is, if we enacted it better, that would be more helpful than amateur innovations.

Our parish does not have a communal reconciliation service. Some have it, some don't, and we shouldn't confuse people. I don't give general absolution. I never had cause to do it, and I don't make up a cause to do it. Some important things like sacraments should be standard. There should not be this or that place to go where it's easier.

I don't do it because it's not standard, but it should be done as standard. The sacrament is in little use and will be in even less use. But people have a sense of sin and guilt, and the ordinary individual way is not helpful. So general absolution should be common.

Many don't appreciate the sacrament of penance. It's a mistake to try to talk them into it. We should respect their psychology and the culture we live in. Whatever the reason, the sacrament is not helpful today. Our responsibility is to make it helpful.

But I don't want to be the easy priest people go to. Nor do I want to confuse people with pastoral free-lancing. I do want to make the sacrament work to free people of their guilt.

I am concerned also about the multiplication of anointings of the sick, which priests do at random, sometimes at communal anointings. People are told that if they don't feel good, they should come on up and be anointed. I'm against that. It cheapens the sacrament.

At the same time, I recognize there is a lot of pain and suffering out there. This being so, the church could do a lot of good with a non-sacramental ritual, which it would not pretend is an anointing of the sick.

The Pope

I had great hopes for the pope and find it sad that he seems to feel the need to direct the whole church into his personal piety and persuasion. It's sad because it could be otherwise. A man of his stature and brilliance could be leading us into something great.

But it's not happening, except for his wonderful stance on social justice, which I find groundbreaking and really good. On social issues he is progressive and on target and hopeful. On other issues, I wouldn't say he's regressive, but he's certainly conservative.

It could be he's right. That's the scary thing. But even if he's right, it's better to let it alone and work it out. Some things you let go, others you stop. I don't want to have a contrary opinion of the pope, but I must admit, I do.

The church should take risks, if any institution should. Let's not talk about the pope, but about the church as a whole. The church should be more hopeful. Who else is more protected and inspired? If we don't show hope, who else is supposed to?

We seem so concerned about surviving and staying alive. Jesus came to make us free. We could be so much freer. We have a right to be a free zone in the world. We have the responsibility to be a free zone, not to make more laws. As an institution, we were set free. If we do something bad with our freedom, we have remedies for that. That's what sacraments are for — reconciliation and healing, a whole system of life and joy and hope. Why are we so cautious?

Liberal? Radical?

A liberal thinks people need help; a radical thinks we're all in trouble. I think we're all in trouble, but after twenty-five years I'm more liberal than radical. Not much is achieved by defiance, unless something is obviously wrong. Then we should talk about it, try to change it, or just do what's to be done, as with girl servers.

Some things you have to do on your own — some creative things in marriage, in annulments and the like, using internal forum. But I'm cautious with that. You can't arbitrarily regularize what comes to you. Some look for the easier priest. Others want church recognition, not just what I can give them.

The church is providing that. Annulments are much easier these days. Eighty percent go through. Sociologists would have something to say about that. Why can't someone just say something about divorce, instead of just mucking our way through as we do? If Moses could do something with the Israelites' hard hearts [i.e., grant divorces], the church can do it. It can make some new rules as he did for marriage, because of hardened hearts.

People's lives are hard. Marriage is extremely difficult. How tough it is to have a stable, Christian marriage today. We in the support business tell people, "Do what you can. God understands. The church takes up the slack." How can the church be harder than God? It takes some understanding of frailties.

Authority

I don't fear retaliation from my bishop. He's a just man. There's not much of a problem here. The priests I know do pretty much what they think they must do. There is no need for insubordination.

But I wish there were more creativity among us. One does not have a sense of great urgency. To an extent, we are only keeping the store. I include myself in this. What's missing is liveliness, zeal, fervor. We're in a holding pattern.

I don't know the solution. I'm just reporting. It's not as exciting as in the '60s and '70s. Maybe ennui and confusion have set in. A lot of us don't know what to do. Maybe that's what we are doing now, waiting for the right time.

Fantasy

I can't even visualize the universal hard-line scenario. I don't know what it would mean. Nobody is going to preach on birth control or abortion every week unless you beat him with something. I can't even visualize anyone going to the hard line.

It's true, some seminarians are taking a conservative, non-pastoral, more institutional approach. That's my impression. And people would be less responsive if they thought priests were serving the church rather than them.

But that's more from a priest's personality and theology than from any laying down of rules — I don't know what rules. I don't know what you lay on people any more.

Chapter 29

Fr. Yates and Nell:
A Pastor and His Client

FR. PETER YATES is a pastor in a western diocese with thirty years' experience as a parish priest, twenty-six as a pastor. His parishes have ranged from highly educated professional to low-income inner-city to "urban multicultural."

His bishop kids him in public about being "creative" in his extensive ministry to the divorced and remarried. He would like to write a book about bending the law, but then he wouldn't be able to help people in this way any more. He was quite explicit about the need to protect his identity, lest his ministry to the divorced and remarried come to an end.

He was referred by a woman whose marriage to a divorced non-Catholic he had "blessed." The woman, whom we will call Nell, had gone to him when her own pastor seemed unbending.

He is currently handling fifteen to twenty such cases a year. The number is growing as baby-boomers settle down and get their lives in order, which includes returning to church. Many don't know how to return or have been victimized, he said. Some have tried the annulment process, others have not. "Each case is unique. We must go for the spiritual good of the person."

Fr. Yates has been called in by more than one bishop who asked him, "Did you marry people?" [Understood, outside the law.]

To this "external forum question," Fr. Yates has given an "external answer," namely, "No." The bishops recognized that and were satisfied. "You keep the internal out of the external," he said.

Like Michael Jordan and the basketball commissioner when Jordan was caught gambling?

"Yes," he said. "That's it."

His bishop knows what he's doing, namely, offering a conscientious way out of "bad" marriages by liberal use of the "internal forum" option, that is, through off-the-record approval and even ceremony.

For Fr. Yates, it was a matter of "not bending rules but applying them as they were meant to be applied."

In all this, he draws on his Jesuit, Roman theological education and on the distinction between English common law and Roman law. "People stuck in Anglo-Saxon legalism have a problem with Roman law," he said.

"Bending Roman law is the same as using it. It's a pastoral injustice to make the law more important than one's relationship with Christ and his church."

He urges people to "find the place of law" in their lives, to learn how to "interpret information, be reasonable, be responsible, then do it," that is, do as their informed conscience tells them to do. Those who can take it, let them take it, is his approach.

Rome is upset over the number of annulments granted in the United States, he said. "But some countries do without tribunals entirely — Mexico, for one, where cases are handled at the parish level. The idea is to forgive what's past and celebrate what's present."

He emphasizes "the primacy of grace." Not all lay people appreciate it. Some tell him, "You're bending the law, Father. How do you get away with that?"

One who does not press the point is Nell. The man Nell wanted to marry, Joe, had been married to his first wife by a minister. So it was a valid marriage that had to be annulled. But Joe would have had to write up his personal problems for strangers to read. He and his wife, divorced six years earlier, had no children. He didn't know where she was. Nell and Joe had met three years after his divorce.

An annulment was out of the question. He didn't want to go

through the "awful process"; and Nell didn't want him to. "It was asking too much," she said.

She went to Fr. Yates on a friend's recommendation after approaching her own parish priest, who went by the book. Fr. Yates "blessed the union" in a private church ceremony. Informal as it was, it satisfied Nell's conscience. What Fr. Yates did "was official enough for me," she said.

Afterward, she and Joe went to a judge for an on-record ceremony. All in all, she found this "softer approach" by Fr. Yates "pretty reasonable."

Born into a traditional Catholic family and a product of Catholic schools through college, she approves of Fr. Yates's approach. "I think priests have to do that," she said. "Not everybody fits. It's not fair for the church to ask Joe's involvement in the annulment process, he not Catholic and all. It was pretty hard-nosed."

Hard-nosed maybe, but not continuing, or maybe just not observant, because Nell, now married, returned to the same parish and took up life as a full-fledged member. She had changed her name with marriage and hadn't been active in the parish as a single person. The pastor who had required the annulment probably didn't know her. So she just blended in as a wife and mother, receiving communion as usual.

It's a parish whose bulletin runs a message now and then asking Catholics in bad marriages to inquire about the annulment process. "Need guidance?" the bulletin asks. Nell has never inquired.

She feels there are a lot like her, who have made various compromises. She feels as Catholic as anybody else. Sometimes she wonders if she should be going to holy communion and feels a little bit "in limbo" sometimes — her phrase, partial proof of her Catholic upbringing. "But not often," she said, "and nobody ever asks."

Ironically, she had further experience of her priest's going by the book when she brought her and Joe's baby daughter to be baptized a year or so after their private wedding.

For one of the godparents, she named a lapsed Catholic friend. The woman, "religious and a good person," had joined her husband's Protestant congregation. But Nell's pastor required the woman to produce testimony from a Catholic parish as to her being a member in good standing, and needless to say she couldn't produce it. So she served instead as "something else, a Christian witness perhaps," Nell recalled.

The other godparent produced the required testimony but couldn't be there for the baptism. So Nell asked her father, a pillar of his parish in another state, to stand in for the missing godparent. But the pastor said he also had to prove his good standing.

"I put my foot down then," said Nell, and the baptism went as planned without her father's parish verifying his Catholicism.

"It seemed they were making it awfully difficult to baptize this little baby," she said.

Later, sometime after the baptism, Nell and Joe moved to another neighborhood. The priest, informed of the change of address, told her she would have to change parishes. But she liked it there, even with this fellow in charge. So they stayed anyhow. Their daughter attends Sunday School and has made her first communion there.

Before the first communion, Nell checked with a nun of the parish whether her non-Catholic friends might attend, among them Joe, and was told, "Fine." Joe not only attended but helped bring up offertory gifts during mass. He did not receive communion, however. "I wouldn't want him to do that," said Nell, who has her own standards.

Chapter 30

Una and the Tribunal:
One Woman's Experience

NELL SKIPPED ANNULMENT; Una went through the process. Divorced and seeking to marry Nat, she went through the tribunal of a Midwestern diocese. Una (not her real name) described her experience.

She and her first husband had seen a priest when they realized their marriage was in trouble. He gave them ideas on improving communication with each other. They only saw him once, however. Later they decided to separate and divorce, and that was the end of talking to priests for a while.

Over a year after the divorce, Una and Nat met and in due time decided to marry. She went to her parish to seek an annulment, meeting several times with the parish priest. He asked about her first husband, how long they had known each other, how they had decided to marry, what their relationships had been with their respective families. In this way he got a read on the situation. After several visits, they got down to what Una thought had gone wrong.

The priest also explained what an annulment was. It was not, as she had thought, that you were never married. People had said to her, "How can you get one if you have children?" thinking it made them illegitimate.

The priest told her the church would recognize it as a marriage, and a record of it would remain on her baptismal certificate. The church would not say there had been no marriage, but that something had been missing.

She and the priest went over questions from the ceremony, as to whether she acted of her free will and the like. He pressed her on her case for annulment, taking her through forms she had to fill out at the parish level, which she considered "not a lot." Then he sent the papers downtown.

Downtown there was more paperwork and meetings and psychological tests, "to see if I was sane — they didn't say that, but it's what I felt it was."

Once downtown, she had no more contact with the parish priest — not even later, when there were delays. When she wondered how things were going, she called downtown.

The process went in stages, which were months apart. Witnesses filled out "voluminous" paperwork. There were interviews and another waiting period. Then more tests. She was not told how they were evaluated or what was decided from them.

An older priest, not in good health, handled her case. She was told that much of the delay, which was considerable, was caused by his bad health. "He was out sick months and months. Nobody picked up on his workload." It struck Una, a middle manager, as "a totally ridiculous system."

When the archdiocese said there was no fee, but they would like a $300 donation, Una was told by friends who had gotten annulments that it would take longer if she didn't make the donation. She had also heard you could get it quicker if you upped the donation. She gave $300.

It took eighteen months. A brother of a friend filed for annulment "many months" after she did and got it in two months — "which led me to wonder about the whole process," she said.

A priest friend with tribunal experience helped. They tried to reserve a day for the marriage "just in case" but couldn't. Nat called the priest with tribunal experience, who said he'd do that as a favor — schedule them "in case." He said not to worry. He then made some phone calls. The annulment arrived "days" before the wedding.

Knowing of some others, like a couple married twenty years with six children who got an annulment, Una thinks "they make it up as they go." For her it was "one of the most horrendous processes" of her life. "You'd probably get a whole different story from the two-month man," she said.

A year or so later, she received a mailed survey questionnaire from the diocese, seeking comment on the process. She gladly filled out pages of information, citing "miscommunication, lack of information, and delay."

It's one thing, she said, if you know it's going to take a year. It's another to be told, "We don't know" or "Don't you understand? Father's out sick."

"We got the impression we were out of line questioning them," she said. "But the only reason I kept calling was that I didn't have any information and they wouldn't tell me."

Chapter 31

Bishop McManus:
From Golden Pond

BISHOP WILLIAM E. MCMANUS is retired after twenty-six years a bishop and fifty-four years a priest. He headed Catholic schools for the Chicago archdiocese, worked in Washington for the U.S. bishops, was a pastor in Chicago, and headed the Fort Wayne–South Bend diocese.

Now he lives in a small house on a suburban side street, performing a ministry with unwed mothers, engaged couples, and others. Most of the couples are members of the parish to which he belongs. Some come from a Chicago parish where he was a pastor some years back.

He considers himself a free-lancer, living "the adventurous life of an episcopal tramp." He has his card ready wherever he goes, in case someone needs him for preaching or parish work or giving retreats or days of recollection. He gives a talk or invocation at the drop of a hat.

These have been the best years of his priesthood, he says. "No administrative duties. I just have to keep this house clean." Spare and slight, he listened carefully and answered generously every question, even some that might make a prelate cringe. On a quiet fall afternoon in his living room, he had a lot to say.

Birth Control

In this room in the last nine years, I have prepared forty or so couples for marriage, in eight-hour sessions. If the couple doesn't bring up contraception, I do, because it's essential to compatibility for them to understand church teaching and to know each other's reaction to it.

I say, "The two of you must come to an understanding about spacing children and how to cope with the moral situation involved with it." I don't ask them to put it on the line to me, but I put it to them. Their respect for me is stronger if I tell the church position. In the interests of truth, I also tell them of moralists who disagree, like Fr. Richard McBrien in his book *Catholicism*. The book has an imprimatur. Nothing in it is contrary to faith and morals. It lays out the teaching and dissents.

I say, "Above all, be conscientious about it. Be guided not by what others do, or solely by economic considerations, or by what friends tell you. Ask yourselves what God expects of you in your circumstances and face that situation squarely."

Abortion

Perhaps because of the sheltered life I have led in my administrative haven, I have not met many women who had abortions or contemplated having them. At Fort Wayne, at the prodding of Fr. Terry Place, my vicar general, I initiated a counseling program for women who had undergone abortions. It offered professional guidance to help overcome the harrowing guilt that often follows. This was future protection for a child yet to be conceived, recognizing what got the mother into the situation in the first place.

A woman in a mood of despair and despondency is much more likely to have an abortion than one who has been able to cope with a serious problem of her past. Guilt precipitates people into doing the very evil they are guilty about. So we tried to lift guilt, so they might aspire to virtue as a new value in their lives. We made a pointed effort to regain what you would call mental health, after the trauma of an abortion.

No women have come to me who said, "I am thinking of having an abortion because of rape or incest or because the doctor warned that my life is threatened." Statistics indicate there are such cases. A common client of an abortion clinic is a woman already a mother, who comes often under great pressure from her immediate family.

I have had peripheral experience in this matter. Since I re-tired, I have taken a group of single mothers under my wing, a support group. All are clients of Catholic Charities. It's an ad-ministrator's dream: no name, no bylaws, no constitution, no mission statement, no schedule. Simply friends.

I've gotten to know, admire, and love these mothers. They told me their stories. Each was seriously tempted to abortion in their first three months of pregnancy. In the second three, they considered adoption. In the last three, bonding set in, and they had no other thought than to keep the child, no matter the difficulties.

There are enormous difficulties. One-third of their gross in-come goes for day care, while they work. Any recreation costs triple because of the need for childcare. These are heroic people.

I had a party here Sunday after baptizing the latest arrival in my group. The mother had been orphaned at seven, then was raised by a grandmother, who put her through Catholic schools. The grandmother died. Virtually alone and particularly attrac-tive, she hooked up with a fellow on drugs and alcohol who got her pregnant. I baptized her baby, Sean.

She's gonna make it. The agency will pay her rent for a year in a one-room Uptown apartment, provided she is moving from welfare to employment. She has to find a sitter and live on the $20,000 a year she makes waitressing.

I always say the answer to abortion is not bumper stickers but a live baby. We have to facilitate the birth of these babies, not be judgmental. We can go on forever saying a girl should not get pregnant. She *is* pregnant; she's carrying a baby. If we focus attention on the baby, we create an environment that gives the baby a chance, maybe through adoption.

If not, if the mother keeps the child, she needs a lot of one-to-one intervention. Not more agencies. They're all agency-crazy as it is, with food stamps, green card, and the rest. They have to know every conceivable source of aid to make it. Otherwise they have to go on welfare altogether. It's a perpetual dilemma whether they would do better on welfare or working.

Four of these mothers have married. They support each other, staying in touch by phone. You don't need a lot of ma-chinery for something like this. It propels itself. You need just one person to keep a list.

Marriage and Divorce

There are marriages that have reached a point of mere coexis-
tence. They are on the rocks. I refer these couples to counselors.
At that point it's a professional's job, and a long process at that. I
give the couples religious reasons for seeking professional help.

Then there's the marriage that is busted for infidelity, as
when the husband is chasing another woman. There's no hope
of putting it together, so damaged is it by his adultery and
ongoing sexual association with another woman. I tell such a
woman she can leave him, remain separate, and go to court to
obtain legal immunity from him. I refer her to a lawyer and have
her keep coming back to me along the way.

We don't talk annulment until after a divorce. At that time,
I look into whether there's a case, then fill out forms and send
them to the tribunal. I stay with the case to the final decision.

It's always painful trying to get a couple to see the distinction between an annulment and a divorce. We are all bottom-
line-minded: if it's all over and they are free to marry, what's
in a name? I say again and again, divorce says the marriage no
longer is, annulment that it never was. They are not impressed.

There is considerable suspicion about the process, particularly by those who can't get one. Those who get one are all for
it. The approaching marriage is what their minds are set on, that
or peace of mind from being no longer attached to the former
spouse.

The Kennedy in-law who protested her ex-husband's seeking
an annulment is wrong, but I see her point of view. She sees annulment as making her children illegitimate. But the church has
a longstanding legal position that the child is not illegitimate
because of the discovery of a flaw in the marriage, only if the
couple did not even try to be married.

If the evidence at the tribunal says there was no marriage,
there was no marriage. But in the course of collecting evidence,
she has the services of a defender of the marriage bond. She
has the right to hear reasons brought by the one seeking the
annulment and can insist on the permanence of her marriage.

I have high respect for tribunal workers. It's mental torture
for a priest to try to get people squared away with the Lord and
at the same time uphold the law and the institution of marriage.

Altar Girls and Women

Women testifying at hearings before the bishops' committee writing the pastoral on women and society, which was never published, revealed much deep-seated resentment. They spoke of discrimination against them, including coming down so hard on them when sexual ethics are promulgated.

It's been "Women should not have an abortion," when most abortions are performed by men, for instance. Men are making good money at it. Very few women physicians do abortions. So the actual destruction is in the hands of men, but rarely do we come down on doctors who do it, at least in public statements. It's the Eve Complex. Eve led Adam into sin. That sort of thing.

And there's resentment of the church's toleration of discriminatory patterns, as in a pastor saying, "We have to get out a mailing. Let's gather a group of women." Why not men? The church has picked up on the German "children, kitchen, church" complex.

The more militant at these hearings were very strong on the altar-girl ban, which they said makes no sense. If little boys are doing chores around the sanctuary, why not little girls?

And a great many, particularly nuns, were vehement on ordination of women.

I conclude from all this that we should listen to these voices or run the great danger of losing these women. It seems that many women have left the church or cooled off on it. If the baby boomers are lost, what about their children, the busters, the fifteen-to-twenty-five age group?

The ban on altar girls is not reasonable. Is a priest to enter the fourth-grade classroom and ask which boys want to be servers? As bishop of Fort Wayne–South Bend, I just looked the other way. So did Cardinal Bernardin. After making a reasonable thrust affirming the ban in a letter to priests, he backed off when priests protested. He was not about to sacrifice his moral authority on this issue.

The pope — very soon, I think — will make the very insubstantial change in canon law needed to make perfectly legal what is going on almost everywhere in Chicago. The law is that only men can be installed in the ministries of acolyte and lector. But lay women may perform the lector's functions. So just add "and acolyte," thus permitting them to perform the acolyte's functions too. Add a couple of words, and everything will be legal.

I would much prefer to see adults perform such ministries anyway. Yes, perhaps kids are drawn to the priesthood by serving mass. But we want to become more an adult church. And both of those offices historically are full-fledged ministries, to be held in high honor. The adult acolyte with some functions restored and enriched would make a better mass-server. Youngsters are often distracted.

Regarding ordination of women, I'm obedient. The pope asked U.S. bishops not to be advocates, so I'm not. I also say, very honestly, that if the pope were to grant permission and I were an active bishop, I would be right up front in ordaining women.

We hurt the priesthood by limiting it to male celibates. That's a very small segment of humanity from which to draw for the exalted position of being a priest. I would like to see the day when priests are the best people.

I would like to see single and married men and women at the altar because of their qualifications — their piety, dedication, knowledge, skill, and the rest. I know so many nuns who would be extraordinary priests, far more than some young fellows who are ordained — nuns with twenty-five years' experience, with a well-rounded spiritual life, articulate. They stayed with it when walking out was so easy. They are some of the most loyal people in the world, in the forty-to-fifty age bracket. They are doing extraordinary ministries and would make extraordinary priests. But...I will be obedient.

Gays and Lesbians

I have priest friends who are homosexuals. I know because they have confided in me. They take their homosexuality and put it under the same restraints I put my heterosexuality under, living beautifully celibate lives. Most are closet homosexuals. I'm sure I have other friends who are homosexual, and I don't know they are. I have empathy toward them and those to whom they minister. Evidence is mounting that it's a largely genetic phenomenon, an inclination born right into them. There's nothing you can do about it. It's the way you emote. My attitude is one of compassion. It must be very difficult.

Liturgy

Eucharistic [mass] rubrics are to be observed strictly. But there are more options within them than are normally exercised. I came down on priests in Fort Wayne–South Bend for not using options, for being mechanical. There are four Eucharistic prayers and nine prefaces, for instance. But they use the same ones Sunday after Sunday, not relating each to the gospel of the day. Prayers of the faithful and announcements after mass are usually canned. It's sickening.

I did not lose my cool when some sisters had a liturgical dance, which they called interpretive prayer. Nor do I now. Recently at her final vows, Sister Margie broke into a beautiful dance in the convent chapel while the choir sang the Magnificat. When she finished, no one applauded. They had been praying with her. She just sat down again in the front pew with her parents.

I have always distinguished between Eucharistic liturgies and paraliturgies. In a paraliturgy we can do what we want, as long as it's not irreverent and bizarre. For years in Fort Wayne and South Bend, we had a Halloween liturgy for fourth-grade youngsters, one in each of the two cathedrals.

The kids came dressed as saints. We kept things moving, because their span of attention is short. They enthusiastically praised God at one point, bowed their heads in sorrow at another, brought canned food for the poor in a procession to the mayor at another, and heard a Bible reading and song. None of it's in the book. We created it out of whole cloth.

The Pope

Disloyal? First of all, as a bishop, I'm pledged to loyalty, and I believe in keeping pledges. I have been twenty-six years a bishop under two popes. Who am I to voice a word of criticism of those who have had to cope with such enormous responsibilities? What does a pope do at end of day? According to the author Peter Hebblethwaite, he worries.

This present pope is an absolute charmer. It's a thrill to meet him. I have sat across from him at lunch and gotten into a typical clerical discussion about general absolution. The rule is you can give it if people have to wait a long time to be heard individually. What's a long time? He said, "I don't know," putting up his hands. I used that as argument against the one month the U.S. bishops have decreed, which I think they got out of the sky. Cardinal O'Connor of New York responded: "Then we should help the pope."

Two years ago, on my way back from my niece's wedding in Florence, my sister and sister-in-law and I stopped in Rome and saw the pope. He and I concelebrated mass in a private chapel. Afterward, he greeted us and gave the women rosaries, and we all had our picture taken. It was as if he had no other interest in the world. He has a talent for that, making people feel he has no interest in anyone else. He does it before a crowd, maybe drawing on his acting skill.

This pope, like the one before him, is a reflection of his advisors. This is much evident in his latest encyclical, *Veritatis Splendor.* One school of moral theology got his ear. That's common knowledge; so there will be controversy swirling around that encyclical.

Like Pope Paul VI he is holy. He prays and prays hard. No one has ever questioned that. He's a man of profound spirituality and prayer, trying to make decisions as he sees them.

But when he visited the United States, he didn't come with the view of learning anything. A bishop who traveled with him on the plane the whole trip said he didn't ask a question. He was wired for sound, all prepared. Maybe he has to be, giving twenty or thirty speeches from city to city. But he really does not have the collegial pattern, which is extremely important for governance of the church.

The world synod of bishops hasn't turned out as envisioned, as a real forum. The U.S. doesn't need a representative to the Vatican but the U.S. Conference of Bishops does, so that when letters and tirades arrive from the conservative newspaper *The Wanderer,* the Vatican will know how to interpret them.

Such a representative could counter negative attitudes the pope may have toward the U.S., which he has heard from people who have his ear but sometimes know only what they have heard. It would be someone ineligible for Vatican appointment or for anything better back home, someone to keep the top people informed, so we would not wait six years to hear about girl servers, for instance.

Liberal? Radical?

I take my stand issue by issue. Most bishops do. Some symptoms creep up now and then, showing left and right leanings. But great inconsistencies too. Every bishop is entitled to his own opinion. Retired bishops have voice but not vote. The joke now, since I've been rather articulate as a retired bishop, whatever my mood happens to be, is to restore my vote and take away my voice.

I worked for the bishops' conference eleven years as staff [assistant director of the education department of what was then the National Catholic Welfare Conference, or NCWC]. The conference's name came from the initials. Toward the end of World War I, the bishops formed the National Catholic War Council, to support the war effort. They saved the logo and made it welfare instead of war.

But the word "council" implied jurisdiction over them, some bishops complained. This was unthinkable in those days. So it was changed to conference, after being wholly suppressed for a time. Even now the only votes that bind all are those dealing with liturgy and seminary curriculum. It's looser even than a confederation.

Authority

As I said, I am pledged to obedience to the pope, and I take that seriously. When I ordain a priest, he kneels before me and promises obedience to me and my successors. I did it fifty-four years ago, to Cardinal George Mundelein in '39, the last class he ordained.

Most priests are quite faithful to this. There are differences, then a showdown. As bishop, you discuss it and make a decision and present it. In my experience priests obey it. I encountered very little defiance.

But I told them over and over, "I'm not a policeman. Be as creative and resourceful as you can. Don't be afraid to make mistakes. If everything is regulated, we stultify ourselves. Inaction results." That worked rather well. There was some mistrust, some of it generated by laity, particularly on financial matters.

We had a rule that parishes had to deposit their money with the chancery, like a co-op, which made loans for capital improvements, etc. The rule was to keep one month's supply, send the rest to Fort Wayne. Well, subterfuge ensued.

Bank certificates of deposit were paying 10 percent to 13 percent. The diocese was paying 3 percent but was lending at 4 percent. Banks were charging prime, which was 15 percent. After much subterfuge, hidden bank accounts, etc., I decided to give each parish an ordinary bank book showing deposits and withdrawals. The bankbooks were something they could use to provide visible assurance to the laity. If you wanted to withdraw, you could, any time. It worked. Money poured in, a half million dollars in a short time.

Aside from that episode, my priests and I had pretty good rapport.

Do I fear retaliation? No. Reprimand maybe. There's a difference. I've been reprimanded a few times by Rome but very gently.

The Fantasy

A couple anecdotes about the fantasy. One of the best lessons I ever had was from a twelve-year-old girl who came to me with her problem: Her parents had forbidden her to play with a black blind girl whom the family next door had taken in as a foster child.

"My parents say, stay away," she told me. "But she has no playmate, and I have decided to play with her anyhow, because I think that's what God wants me to do."

The whole picture should be considered. Her parents were alarmed about the black child in their all-white neighborhood. They didn't want to be pilloried by their neighbors. The young lady wanted to be obedient but felt she had to take a totally countercultural action.

"Did I do right?" she asked me.

"You sure did," I said.

The point: as moral theology develops, it will point out more right things to do and will say less about wrong things. In the seminary I picked up a whole catalog of all the sins that could be committed, but learned very little about virtue. We need scenarios as I just gave you, of how you can practice virtue.

I would like to revise the ritual of confession to include a recitation, up front, of good things you have done. Our people are looking for ways to be good but are quite clumsy in how to do them. When the church shows them, they become very attached to the church. On the other hand, if we incessantly condemn evil that happens anyway, we are just making noises that don't register anywhere.

The more the church is ignored when it condemns these evils, the more it loses its potential for pointing out what's good. Take a stand, as on contraception. Then let it go at that. Everyone knows what the church holds. Let's start talking about the things that are intrinsically right. Marriage encounter, for instance. Get everyone in. And let's have couples intervene for these single mothers, take personal interest in them for the rest of their lives. We have to go for the good.

The second anecdote: the Indiana constitution prohibited gambling. In 1976, when I arrived, penny poker was a misdemeanor. But big gambling was going on everywhere, in barber shops and the like — a million and a half a year on sports, a sports reporter told me.

There was bingo everywhere. One parish held a Super Las Vegas afternoon on a Sunday, women carrying trays of steins to tables, everyone having a hilariously good time. A reporter got in, and next day there was a blazing story, "Churchgoers gamble Sunday afternoon," in full detail.

Next morning, the state's attorney was on my back. I knew I had trouble with him. I also knew I had trouble with my conscience. So I went to see a moral theologian to get off the hook. I didn't want to ban gambling. People were having fun, it was not unethical, no gangs were running it. It was perfectly ethical but illegal.

I went to the University of Notre Dame and saw Enda McDonagh, a visiting professor from a seminary in Ireland, and said, "Get me off the hook. How can I do this and still have a peaceful conscience?"

He said, "You can't" and told me why. "This is a law," he said. "The state has the right to make it. A violation could be excused for an extraordinarily good reason, but raising money for the church would be the worst reason you could cite."

We were insisting on enforcement of the pornography law, so we couldn't flout this law. We could try to get rid of the gambling law, but meanwhile we should observe it. "You have a year to get rid of it all," he told me. "Ease the bingo out. In a year you should be clean."

It was a serious matter, he said, my moral obligation. I put it to my priests and the other bishops of the state. They scoffed at it. But I banned gambling in the diocese. I am hated to this day for it. We found other money sources. Meanwhile, I denounced the state law every chance I got. It took six years and two general assemblies before they got rid of it.

Moral theology covered the whole situation. It told me to do more than pay the penalty if I was caught. McDonagh looked at the whole picture, even gave me a schedule. That's good moral theology, the best kind of direction. The whole thing was providential. It brought about social change. He said it would. "If you do this," he said, "the law will be changed."

Those are two rather copious anecdotes about how moral theology can work positively rather than negatively. With that emphasis will come good news, which is what Catholics crave.

Now we have bad news: sexual abuse by clergy, financial difficulties, controversies of one sort or another, politicization of bishops' appointments, and on and on. Ugly problems, greatly exaggerated by excessive secrecy.

People are waiting for headlines like "Pope Relaxes. It's Okay to Use Girls as Servers. Permission Granted."

After such news there would be great exultation, as there was after Vatican II or when foolish laws were abolished, like midnight fasting and Lenten fasting rules.

Or the good news might be that the pope seeks counsel from a bishop. Anything the bulk of Catholics would classify as good news would be good news for the church.

The vision I have is an awakening that makes us a gospel

church. "Gospel" is another word for good news. A change from what we are now, an institutional church.

We need the spirit of openness that John XXIII advocated and a lot of proclamation of good news. Then we will see a revival.

Chapter 32

What Theologians Say

I F THERE ARE PRIESTS who soften the Vatican hard line, where do they find support for their position? Preeminently among theologians, specifically those who deal with so-called moral theology, or, to use a term more common to Protestants, "Christian ethics." These moral theologians pick their way through the morass of directions issued by church authority over the centuries, trying to discover what matters and what doesn't.

They operate in a sort of world of their own — though no more than lawyers and doctors — talking a specialized language and trying to solve a specified set of problems. They address issues largely peculiar to Catholics, who stand on or bear the weight of a long tradition. Still these Catholic moralists — another common term — look beyond Catholic circles to their "separated brethren" and sometimes collaborate with them.

In large part, however, the moralists talk to the Catholic community. Like professionals anywhere, much of their talking is to each other. But what they say trickles down or boils over into journals and magazines that priests read and is discussed in conferences and seminars. They are the professionals to whom working pastors often turn for their continuing education. What these professionals are saying backs up the priests who buck the Vatican and seem to bend rules. Here is a look at what the moralists are saying, which priests read and which then trickles down or boils over even further to the daily lives of Catholic parishioners.

Take Richard A. McCormick, the Jesuit who for nineteen years, from 1965 to 1984, did a regular critical roundup of what moralists were saying, "Notes on Moral Theology," in the distinguished Jesuit-edited quarterly *Theological Studies*.

McCormick is a major figure in today's discussion of moral questions. A moral theologian of world-class dimensions, he has been one of the leaders toward a more nuanced understanding of what the law requires. He is one of those who lend justification to benders of the law, though in his meticulous, nuanced prose he would never use the phrase, nor perhaps find it useful.

His is the pursuit of precision rather than flexibility. But seeking precision, he makes distinctions meant to withstand the bright light of peer review and criticism. He belongs to a priesthood of its own, academic theology, but with a decided practical, one might say lawyerly, slant. When McCormick talks, church people listen, some to damn, some to be guided.

He is in a class by himself among U.S. moral theologians, according to John A. Gallagher in his 1990 book *Time Past, Time Future: An Historical Study of Catholic Moral Theology*. Nobody "has contributed as much to contemporary American discussions of the development of moral theology," wrote Gallagher, who called McCormick "a scholar steeped in the tradition and sensitive to current developments within it." His "Notes on Moral Theology" provided "a sort of clearinghouse for issues pertinent to moral theology."

Through these "Notes" and journal articles, McCormick brought European thinking to Americans while grappling with American problems and learning Protestant theologies. The latter made him sensitive to "Protestant dimensions of American culture," something Gallagher made bold to characterize as "not fundamentally inimical to a Catholic way of life."

Here are some ideas and trends charted by McCormick in the early 1980s, as he was winding down his *Theological Studies* performance with fifteen years to look back on in the field. The working pastor has been given much to chew on, whether from McCormick or from other writers.

Disillusionment

For one thing, the pastor has been given cause to wonder about the quality of Catholic leadership, as demonstrated in the 1980 Rome synod, a gathering of a representative sample of bishops from around the world. These bishops joined the pope in reaffirming the anti-birth-control position and continued to uphold excommunication of divorced and remarried couples, though recommending "gradualism" as a pastoral approach to these problems.

They did so even while several national bodies of bishops were calling for a study of these two issues "at the highest levels." In addition, arrayed against them was "a heavy majority of theologians," said McCormick, who found the bishops' behavior "theologically and pastorally disturbing, to say the very least."

At the synod itself, some dissented. The archbishop of San Francisco, John R. Quinn, said in the presence of the pope himself, who could not have been happy to hear it, that most priests and theologians do not accept the "intrinsic evil of each and every use of contraception." (In other words, sometimes it's okay.) These objectors were people "whose learning, faith, discretion and dedication to the Church [were] beyond doubt," said Quinn, who proposed worldwide dialogue between the pope and theologians and defended "doctrinal development" (change) as a longstanding "principle and fact."

Quinn said the birth-control problem would not be solved by simply repeating the condemnation. He argued for the doctrinal development he had in mind with references to Bible scholarship and religious liberty; on both of these issues, the church had changed its position.

Quinn wasn't the only bishop to speak up. Cardinal G. Emmett Carter of Toronto suggested that lay resistance to papal teaching on birth control might be a case of the Holy Spirit speaking to the church (!). Cardinal George B. Hume of England added that married people's views must be considered in this matter.

Regarding the divorced and remarried, Archbishop Derek Worlock of Liverpool said his discussions with Liverpool Catholics before the synod did not support the "scandal" notion, which was invoked to keep divorced and remarried from communion.

Canadian bishops later told Canadian Catholics that bishops at the synod had called for "a new and far-reaching study" on pastoral care for the divorced and remarried. "Many bishops" wanted continuing research toward "a new and fuller presentation of what is involved in this question," the Canadians said.

Be that as it may, the synod in its final statements upheld the old way. This is what McCormick found "disturbing."

In addition, the synod deck was stacked with lay people speaking in favor of the approved "natural family planning," a sophisticated form of the rhythm method, the Jesuit Thomas Reese noted in *America*, a readily available Catholic journal. Dissenting bishops did not want to be reported as challenging the pope, Reese reported.

The *Tablet*, a London newspaper widely read on both sides of the Atlantic, called the synod a case of "foregone conclusions virtually imposed on a so-called consultative body." In other words, it was not something your garden-variety thoughtful pastor was likely to take seriously.

McCormick let his impatience show. "I used to believe that closer cooperation between bishops and theologians might solve many of our pastoral problems and foster the credibility of the church's teaching office," he wrote. Not if they don't speak "their true mind" after such consultation, he said, implying that theologians like himself waste their time in such an exercise.

"What is needed," said Bernard Cooke in *Commonweal*, another readily available publication, "is open and careful discussion [by] all responsible voices in the church."

The American Jesuit Avery Dulles alluded (somewhat wryly, it would seem) to a "third magisterium," or teaching authority, after bishops and theologians, namely, church members who cannot separate what has to be believed ("the deposit of faith") from "traditional formulations." These Catholics, said Dulles, feel that "liberal theologians are betraying the faith." These "simple and devout believers," as McCormick called them, pressure bishops, who pressure theologians or at least get testy with them.

"Who will rid me of this troublesome priest?" King Henry

asks his court in "A Man for All Seasons"; and out went the roughneck nobles to do Becket in. Apparently, bishops get the same way about theologians, though without such bloody results.

It's a shame, said Joseph Fuchs, a German Jesuit, the result of mistaking unity in faith for unity in moral teachings. Catholics can disagree on some moral issues, said Fuchs.

Popes have not always agreed with each other, though they have been loath to admit it. For instance, John Paul II recognized a "social mortgage" on private property, thus clearly limiting the rights of the property holder. But his nineteenth-century predecessor Leo XIII, of the encyclical *Rerum Novarum* fame, defended private property as "an almost metaphysical right." The change represents a perfectly respectable evolution, but John Paul apparently did not feel free to acknowledge it, because in his *Laborem Exercens,* where he spoke of the social mortgage, he claimed support by earlier popes in general for his positions.

There has been clearly a rise in disagreement among Catholics in the last thirty years. Before the Second Vatican Council in the 1960s, there was more concern for certainty than for truth, said McCormick. Ironically, among theologians who complained of this, Fuchs pointed out Josef Ratzinger (who had a change of heart himself and later as a cardinal became chief doctrinal policeman under John Paul II).

McCormick had high praise for *Laborem Exercens* ("On Human Work"). It presented an inspiring vision, something to strive for and talk about, rather than a sequence of dos and don'ts. In this encyclical about social justice, John Paul got into the trenches with people trying to solve tough problems.

McCormick wished that church officials in general were less edict-prone and more inclined to persuasion. He cited a "little gem of an essay" by a British writer, Quentin de la Bedoyere, who said the way the church teaches is geared to producing either conformists or rebels, people "who have broken away dramatically from the moral order."

Even *Laborem Exercens* labored, if we may say so, under the disability of being one man's effort. So was the famous *Quadragesimo Anno,* issued by Pius XI in 1931. The difference was that John Paul probably wrote his own encyclical, while Pius XI used a ghost writer, the German Jesuit Oswald von Nell-Breuning.

Nell-Breuning later regretted that worldwide doctrine should have been expressed by him acting alone.

Whether on one's own or using a ghost writer, this process is no way to express the mind of the church as a whole, argued McCormick. It is neither consultative nor collaborative, as it should be, and so produces a "magical" papal authority. To such authority is assigned a "more unearthly character" than to the four Gospels, which scholars routinely dissect for sources and styles, fully recognizing the human process of writing and editing. If we can critique the Gospels, we can do the same for encyclicals, McCormick seems to say.

Priests' Dilemma

Faced with contradictory exercises of authority and perhaps tempted to disillusionment, the garden-variety thinking priest-pastor faces a dilemma. Archbishop Quinn at the 1980 synod talked of "grave personal problems for priests," whose identity is at stake as they function both as representatives of Catholic teaching authority and as pastors of souls.

The more theologically aware the priest is, said Quinn, the more he knows of the widespread disagreement with the papal argument against birth control. As "a man of the church," he is loyal but at the same time knows that "the intellectual foundations" of what he is supposed to defend have been "profoundly eroded."

So eroded had they been by the early 1980s that a French magazine seeking Catholic theologians to discuss sexual matters, on which their church had so much to say, could find no takers. They were keeping their distance from this hottest of topics. But such distance was a luxury the working pastor could not always afford.

What was the pastor to say, unable to decline comment when asked directly by parishioners or faced with a case of conscience? For one thing, the pastor was "no mere courier" from Rome, said a French writer, Andre Naud. Rather, he had "the right and duty" to reflect on official edicts and make his own "responsible contribution to the teaching of the church."

Not for him should be the "politics of silence," which the German Jesuit Karl Rahner had recommended in 1968, advising preachers and teachers to hold back in the face of "provisional" albeit authoritative pronouncements. Not even Rahner, whom McCormick characterized as "the church's foremost theologian, a conservative in the authentic sense of the term," would have said that in 1980.

For one thing, he was on record as saying that "traditional formulations" of noninfallible papal teaching had been "often in error." Indeed, said Rahner, the ten cardinals of the Vatican watchdog agency, the Congregation for the Doctrine of the Faith, "nichts von Theologie verstehen" (knew nothing of theology).

So theologians were to supply "nuance" to Vatican statements on sexual morality, rather than the "religious submission of mind and will" required by the Vatican. This requirement of submission was itself "not sufficiently nuanced" as a description of theologians' role, said Rahner. Part of the problem was the "rather large" number of cases of "unjustified restraint" on theologians that he had witnessed.

Rahner wanted to shorten the grace period of "obsequious silence" in the face of noninfallible edict — a sort of statute of limitation — after which dissent would become legitimate. After all, noted McCormick, even the pope was using terms that not long before had been forbidden, as in his reference to "yahwist authorship" of the Bible, a once-anathema phrase of Bible scholarship.

If the Vatican were serious about prohibiting dissent, why did it put up with so much of it in the wake of the 1968 anti-birth-control statement by Pope Paul VI? It leads one to ask who was practicing "politics of silence" in those years.

McCormick wondered whether the quest for certainty had got out of hand. "Several centuries of high casuistry" had produced a "mechanizing and quantifying of moral judgments" and had led Catholics to expect a certainty that would never be there.

Reading this sort of thing, the priest-pastor might well conclude that he had better think for himself when it came to parish work. "Theological positivism" — something is right "because the Church says so" — was no "substitute for moral reasoning," said McCormick. The pastor had to go beyond it, even if it meant contradicting popular versions of Vatican doctrine.

In other words, the good Catholic should stand up and be counted. Otherwise, commented McCormick, Catholics overly expand church authority, especially the pope's, "in matters not decided by Scripture and tradition." Catholics rush to judgment on debatable matters, a judgment all too freely supplied by the official church, eager to assert itself.

Instead there should be "much greater reserve" in defining the pope's role and greater recognition of the role of priests, bishops, and theologians, said Naud, who favored approaching "each adult member [of the church] as adult."

Naud's work "outspokenly represents the convictions of a large segment of the theological community," said McCormick. In other words, the working pastor who stayed up on his theology could not have missed this point of view.

Think for Oneself

More recently, he might have read McCormick's warning in *America* ("Moral Theology in the Year 2000: Tradition in Transition," April 18, 1992) against idolizing church authority — "fundamentalistic magisteriolatry," he called it, giving us all a mouthful. It's "a privileged source of moral enlightenment" for Catholics; but to put it up there with the Blessed Mother is to "breed conformism."

Instead, he recommended a more tentative approach, building from data rather than solely drawing consequences from principles. This tentative approach has been used in bishops' discussion of social issues. In fields where they have no or little competence, they have consulted experts. Not in sexual matters, however. Here they have not welcomed experts or have welcomed them lukewarmly. Instead, Catholic officialdom has jealously guarded its presumed expertise in sex, an area where in view of its celibacy it might be presumed insufficiently versed.

Sterilization, a medical issue directly connected to marital intercourse, is a case in point and a very practical one for Catholic hospitals. Decided on authority, there's no contest — "no doubt, no discussion, only a clear no," said McCormick in 1981. But a University of Munich theologian, Johannes Grundel, had a better idea. Writing in *Stimmen der Zeit*, he noted the widespread lack of conviction among theologians about the church's anti-sterilization argument. Grundel himself found it "no longer convincing" and beyond that felt obliged to present a counter-argument, as it were to test accepted teaching on the matter, as other teaching, later changed, had been similarly tested.

He proceeded to do so, arguing that (a) marital intercourse left open to childbearing was "not an absolute value," (b) intercourse was to serve "the total personal well-being," (c) sterilization, a "physical evil" like any surgery, was not a moral evil "if there [were] correspondingly serious reasons for its performance," and (d) "conflict situations" could arise where sterilization was permissible and even required in Catholic hospitals. Theologically speaking, this was grabbing the bull by the horns, if not by a more sensitive area.

McCormick again hastened to point out that Grundel was not alone, in fact was "representative of very many truly responsible theologians." He also commended Grundel for not taking a "juridical" approach to the problem, in which the deck is stacked against argument of almost any kind. This juridicism "robs theology of its scientific character" and "paralyzes doctrinal development _in principle,_" he said — at its source, you might say. It was important, in other words, not to play the game of those who rest their case primarily if not solely on authority.

It would not do to root one's entire faith in "the pronouncements of authority," said another writer, an Irish Augustinian priest, Gabriel Daly, in _The Tablet._ He was writing against what McCormick called "the kind of religious faith which does not regard itself as . . . accountable to reason." Not McCormick's kind of faith, needless to say. Such a faith, said Daly, creates an atmosphere "in which open enquiry and honest dissent are arbitrarily construed as disloyalty or worse." He further argued that "orthodoxy is meaningless and possibly immoral if it is not the answer to a genuine search for truth." Fighting words.

The "possibly immoral" business struck home for McCormick soon after this, when Pope John Paul II challenged Jesuits' loyalty because they were doing entirely too much inquiring and dissenting. McCormick defended Jesuits' right to accept noninfallible teaching both "docilely and critically." In this vein he cited a fellow Midwestern Jesuit, historian John W. O'Malley, who had written (provocatively) that a papal command to defend error would "at least border on the immoral"!

The working pastor would find food for thought in this. He would also perk up at the advice of German Jesuit Joseph Fuchs, who counseled "appropriate caution and tentativeness" in telling people what's right and wrong. He warned against the impulse to "infallibilize" the ordinary activity of the magisterium. Vatican II reminded lay people not to expect their pastors to have all the answers, said Fuchs. They can't, he said, and that's not their mission anyway.

Divorced and Remarried

It's clear from pastors' comments that divorced and remarried Catholics present a major issue. As with sterilization, if pastors look exclusively to Rome for their lead, they will pursue a hard line indeed.

At the end of the 1980 bishops' synod, for instance, Pope John Paul II reasserted the "traditional practice" of excluding the divorced and remarried from the sacraments. Rome spoke; the issue should have been closed. But it wasn't.

Almost immediately the papal assertion ran into "a virtually unanimous theological opinion" that not all divorced and remarried deserved this treatment, said McCormick, citing a 1981 survey by a Dominican theologian, Gonzalo Gonzalez, who found "increasing theological voices" demanding new pastoral practice "contrary to the established one."

The new pastoral practice called for courage ("audacia"), said Gonzalez, even to the point of recognizing the obligation to nurture a second marriage after the first one has failed. He retreated from the traditional "state of sin" business—the "bad marriage" of the first chapter. Catholics must preserve marital permanence as a "radical" truth, he said, "but [also] the radical character of mercy in the faith community" — just the kind of language used by pastors.

Again, McCormick noted that this was not new. Gonzalez's study reflected theological thinking of the previous ten years, he said. It was noteworthy because it appeared after the pope had reaffirmed the old norm at the synod.

Meanwhile, the Austrian bishops, also after the pope spoke, announced "special conditions" under which the divorced and remarried might be welcomed back into the fold. The official consensus was that they were to be welcomed back if the first marriage was discovered invalid. But even if it weren't, said Bishop Helmut Kratzl, a Vienna auxiliary, there was still "broad consensus" that the couple might come back as man and wife, and not just as brother and sister — a not unusual arrangement required of the divorced and remarried for several decades.

McCormick agreed on the consensus matter, citing a statement to that effect in 1972 by Professor Josef Ratzinger, later head of the Vatican's Congregation for the Doctrine of the Faith.

Even after the 1980 synod, in a noteworthy mixed-signals performance, Ratzinger (quoted by Kratzl) wrote priests noting that the synod had called for more investigation of the matter, even study of the practice of the Eastern Church allowing divorce, "to make our pastoral compassion even more all-embracing."

The synod's basic concern was pastoral anyhow, said the veteran Redemptorist German theologian Bernard Haring. The rules were subordinate to this pastoral imperative. The brother-sister relationship was not to be imposed when this would cause more harm than good — when it would drive people from the church, for instance, or disturb family harmony. Healing was a kind of "household principle" for the church. The future of pastoral practice lay in a "spirit of healing love." That too is pastors' talk.

In any event, McCormick commended Haring for his pastoral insights and sensitivity but had something to add that went beyond sensitivity. He said that in the long run Catholics must rethink the indissolubility of a marriage where "any semblance of a human relationship is irretrievably dead and gone." He cited a recent article, "Rethinking the Indissolubility of Marriage," in the _Catholic Mind,_ a decidedly mainstream pocket-size journal that operates as a sort of high-grade Catholic _Reader's Digest._

Results Orientation, or "Proportionalism"

A cornerstone of McCormick's thinking, and of many other theologians, has been "proportionalism," a results-oriented, big-picture approach to moral problems. Traditional Catholic thinking has emphasized individual actions taken in themselves, apart from circumstances — at least in the sexual realm. Thus masturbation has been an unjustifiable no-no, absolutely forbidden in itself though not always sinful because of other considerations, such as inattention or accident.

Good pastoral practice, like Haring's sensitivity, has for a long time preferred going easy — say, giving the kid a break when he confesses it for the first time or is in the midst of an unshakable habit. But the absolute prohibition has endured at Rome, where habits die hard.

McCormick and others have a better idea: sometimes masturbation might be okay, as when it is used for "sperm-testing in a sterile marriage." This is proposed by a German Jesuit, Peter Knauer, and McCormick agrees with him, though neither quarrels with the prohibition of masturbation in general. They don't recommend it, in other words; but neither do they accept it as an always overriding issue. For the childless couple, for instance, the issue is their inability to have children. So they balance masturbation with this laudable goal, and having children wins out. It's a judgment call.

At issue is whether such a call is ever in order. Knauer, McCormick, and others say it makes sense. What's at stake is what happens "in general and in the long run" — what we might call a big-picture approach to morality. Traditional formulations, on the other hand, judge each action in itself every time. No, the Knauers and McCormicks say, results can justify actions, though not if they are "counterproductive" over the long haul.

It depends what happens. We look to our experience to decide what's good and bad over the long haul. In some areas we are still working it out, said McCormick, who has put in a lot of work on bioethical issues — as in the pros and cons of recombinant DNA research. In other areas we are on our way to a conclusion based on analyzing results, as regarding the morality of war, namely, that war is never justified.

What then of the prohibitions from Rome, which seem to

offer no such nuance, as Karl Rahner would put it? They offer us an "obligatory ideal," said an American Jesuit, John H. Wright — something along the lines of the requirement always to pay one's debts. This debt-paying remains an ideal even for someone who declares bankruptcy and thus avoids paying them. So what the popes have offered on birth control has been an ideal never to be jettisoned but to be violated for good enough reasons.

Wright's article, in *America* magazine, "eloquently" summarized a decade of commentary by theologians on this matter, said McCormick, again pointing out consensus on the matter.

This big-picture approach to morality accepts the conflicts involved in making important decisions. The Vatican, on the other hand, focuses on the individual act and regularly decides it is right or wrong apart from circumstances. So what do Catholics do? They should be faithful but not fundamentalistic, says Wright. That is, they are to preserve the "essential intent and meaning" of a position, rather than "a particular verbal formula."

Do as the popes have done, he said, in accepting freedom of conscience and separation of church and state, for instance, issues on which popes have "modified earlier authoritative statements ... without being unfaithful to their essential intent."

Paul VI presented an "obligatory ideal" when he told the United Nations, "No more war, never," without annulling the church's longstanding theory of the just war. The same for sterilization. "No more sterilization, never," the popes say, without undermining a parallel theory of justified sterilization.

This "No more war" pope is the pope as prophet, exaggerating to make a point, as the British Jesuit John Mahoney put it in his book *The Making of Moral Theology*. The trouble is that some take the pope literally, to their hurt, said Mahoney. One might add that this is where a thinking pastor comes in, to relieve the needless hurt.

Indeed, there has been a long history of "exception-making" in church law, in nearly all cases decided by the *ratio proportionata* (good enough reason) argument that McCormick and the others are accused of running into the ground.

But traditional Catholic moral theology is "profoundly teleological" (results-oriented), as Protestant theologian James Gustafson said in his 1978 book *Protestant and Roman Catholic Ethics*. This results-orientation covers almost everything we do, said the Jesuit Bruno Schuller.

Once there was an accepted obligation to have children, but Pope Pius XII exempted couples from it for "serious reasons," though limiting the methods to periodic abstinence, or rhythm. The "serious reasons" argument has been used often.

McCormick was defending himself and a whole school of moral theologians when he alluded to these matters. They were under attack for wrongheadedness and even disloyalty for picking at and analyzing papal and other official statements. In response, he employed a sort of judo, using the tradition's own weight against its supposed loyalists.

For instance, Pope John Paul II reached into the vocabulary of "so-called 'proportionalists'" when in *Laborem Exercens* he called emigration "a material evil," or "a necessary evil," something only to be tolerated.

Recent History

It's been a stormy thirty years or so for the Catholic Church. In moral theology, where tough issues are debated, there has been a "Copernican revolution," a "sea change," says Lawrence S. Cunningham, head of the University of Notre Dame theology department.

The old "manual" method, a sort of cookbook approach to pastoral counseling and the hearing of confession, was abandoned. Paul VI's encyclical on birth control led to "ferocious debates," pitting traditionalist against innovator, each claiming roots in the past. In the middle of it all raged a fight over situation ethics, which no Catholic would lay claim to but which some used as a club with which to beat others.

The period became a time for priests to decide which side they were on. The priests interviewed in this book have for the most part chosen to bend rules for the sake of their parishioners. They have not made that choice in a vacuum.

References

All but the last of the following generic references are in Richard A. McCormick, S.J., *Notes on Moral Theology, 1981 through 1984* (Lanham, Md.: University Press of America, 1984). McCormick's comments are from the same volume.

The Quinn, Carter, Hume, and Worlock comments at the 1980 synod and the post-synod Canadian bishops' message are all from *Origins*, 1980.

Others are quoted, in order of appearance, as follows:

Dulles from *Proceedings of the Catholic Theological Society of America*, 1980; Fuchs from *Stimmen der Zeit*, 1983 and 1982; de la Bedoyere from *The Tablet*, 1981; Naud from *Science et Esprit*, 1980; Rahner from *Stimmen der Zeit*, 1980; O'Malley from *Studies in the Spirituality of Jesuits*, 1983; Gonzalez from *Ciencia Tomista*, 1981; Kratzl in *Theologisch-praktische Quartalschrift*, 1981; Ratzinger from *Ehe und Ehescheidung*, Munich, 1972; Haring from *Theologie der Gegenwart*, 1981; Knauer from *Theologie und Philosophie*, 1980; Schuller from *Theologie und Philosophie*, 1970.

Cunningham is quoted directly from *Commonweal*, April 19, 1991.